Masterpiec

Stories of Desert Places

Nella Braddy

Alpha Editions

This edition published in 2022

ISBN : 9789356902336

Design and Setting By
Alpha Editions
www.alphaedis.com
Email - info@alphaedis.com

Contents

EDITOR'S NOTE

In these volumes the word *adventure* has been used in its broadest sense to cover not only strange happenings in strange places but also love and life and death—all things that have to do with the great adventure of living. Questions as to the fitness of a story were settled by examining the qualities of the narrative as such rather than by reference to a technical classification of short stories.

It is the inalienable right of the editor of a work of this kind to plead copyright difficulties in extenuation for whatever faults it may possess. We beg the reader to believe that this is why his favorite story was omitted while one vastly inferior was included.

I

THE BARON'S QUARRY*

EGERTON CASTLE

*Reprinted by permission of D. Appleton & Co.

"Oh no, I assure you, you are not boring Mr. Marshfield," said this personage himself in his gentle voice—that curious voice that could flow on for hours, promulgating profound and startling theories on every department of human knowledge or conducting paradoxical arguments without a single inflection or pause of hesitation. "I am, on the contrary, much interested in your hunting talk. To paraphrase a well-worn quotation somewhat widely, *nihil humanum a me alienum est.* Even hunting stories may have their point of biological interest: the philologist sometimes pricks his ear to the jargon of the chase; moreover, I am not incapable of appreciating the subject-matter itself. This seems to excite some derision. I admit I am not much of a sportsman to look at, nor, indeed, by instinct, yet I have had some out-of-the-way experiences in that line—generally when intent on other pursuits. I doubt, for instance, if even you, Major Travers, notwithstanding your well-known exploits against man and beast, notwithstanding that doubtful smile of yours, could match the strangeness of a certain hunting adventure in which I played an important part."

The speaker's small, deep-set, black eyes, that never warmed to anything more human than a purely speculative, scientific interest in his surroundings, here wandered round the sceptical yet expectant circle with bland amusement. He stretched out his bloodless fingers for another of his host's superfine cigars and proceeded, with only such interruptions as were occasioned by the lighting and careful smoking of the latter.

"I was returning home after my prolonged stay in Petersburg, intending to linger on my way and test with mine own ears certain among the many dialects of eastern Europe—anent which there is a symmetrical little cluster of philological knotty points it is my modest intention one day to unravel. However, that is neither here nor there. On the road to Hungary I bethought myself opportunely of proving the once pressingly offered hospitality of the Baron Kossowski.

"You may have met the man, Major Travers, he was a tremendous sportsman, if you like. I first came across him at McNeil's place in remote Ireland. Now, being in Bukowina, within measurable distance of his Carpathian abode, and curious to see a Polish lord at home, I remembered his invitation. It was already of long standing, but it had been warm, born in fact of a sudden fit of enthusiasm for me"—here a half-mocking smile quivered an instant under the speaker's black moustache—"which, as it was characteristic, I may as well tell you about.

"It was on the day of, or rather, to be accurate, on the day after my arrival, toward the small hours of the morning, in the smoking-room at Rathdrum. Our host was peacefully snoring over his empty pipe and his seventh glass of whiskey, also empty. The rest of the men had slunk off to bed. The baron, who all unknown to himself had been a subject of most interesting observation to me the whole evening, being now practically alone with me, condescended to turn an eye, as wide awake as a fox's, albeit slightly bloodshot, upon the contemptible white-faced person who had preferred spending the raw hours over his papers, within the radius of a glorious fire's warmth, to creeping slily over treacherous quagmires in the pursuit of timid bog creatures (snipe shooting had been the order of the day)—the baron, I say, became aware of my existence and entered into conversation with me.

"He would no doubt have been much surprised could he have known that he was already mapped out, craniologically and physiognomically, catalogued with care, and neatly laid by in his proper ethnological box, in my private type museum, that, as I sat and examined him from my different coigns of vantage in library, in dining and smoking room that evening, not a look of his, not a gesture went forth but had significance for me.

"You, I had thought, with your broad shoulders and deep chest, your massive head that should have gone with a tall stature, not with those short, sturdy limbs; with your thick red hair, that should have been black for that matter, with your wide-set, yellow eyes, you would be a real puzzle to one who did not recognize in you equal mixtures of the fair, stalwart, and muscular Slav with the bilious-sanguine, thick-set, wiry Turanian. Your pedigree would no doubt bear me out; there is as much of the Magyar as of the Pole in your anatomy. Athlete, and yet a tangle of nerves; a ferocious brute at bottom, I dare say, for your broad forehead inclines to flatness, under your bristling beard your jaw must protrude, and the base of your skull is ominously thick. And, with all that, capable of ideal transports; when that girl played and sang to-night I saw the swelling of your eyelid veins, and how that small, tenacious, clawlike hand of yours twitched. You would be a fine leader of men—but God help the wretches in your power!

"So had I mused upon him. Yet I confess that when we came into closer contact with each other even I was not proof against the singular courtesy of his manner and his unaccountable personal charm.

"Our conversation soon grew interesting; to me as a matter of course, and evidently to him also. A few general words led to interchange of remarks upon the country we were both visitors in and so to national characteristics—Pole and Irishman have not a few in common, both in their nature and history. An observation which he made, not without a certain flash in his light eyes and a transient uncovering of the teeth, on the Irish type of female beauty, suddenly suggested to me a stanza of an ancient Polish ballad, very full of milk-and-blood imagery, of alternating ferocity and voluptuousness. This I quoted to the astounded foreigner, in the vernacular, and this it was that metamorphosed his mere perfection of civility into sudden warmth, and, in fact, procured me the invitation in question.

"When I left Rathdrum the baron's last words to me were that if I ever thought of visiting his country otherwise than in books he held me bound to make Yany, his Galician seat, my headquarters of study.

"From Czernowicz, therefore, where I stopped some time, I wrote, received in due time a few lines of prettily worded reply, and ultimately entered my sled in the nearest town to, yet at a most forbidding distance from, Yany, and started on my journey thither.

"The undertaking meant many long hours of undulation and skidding over the November snow, to the somniferous bell-jangle of my dirty little horses; the only impression of interest being a weird gipsy concert I came in for at a miserable drinking-booth half buried in the snow where we halted for the refreshment of man and beast. Here, I remember, I discovered a very definite connection between the characteristic run of the tsimbol, the peculiar bite of the Zigeuner's bow on his fiddle-string, and some distinctive points of Turanian tongues—in other countries, in Spain for instance, your gipsy speaks differently on his instrument. But, oddly enough, when I later attempted to put this observation on paper I could find no word to express it."

A few of our company evinced signs of sleepiness, but most of us who knew Marshfield, and that he who could, unless he had something novel to say, be as silent and retiring as he now evinced signs of being copious, awaited further with patience. He has his own deliberate way of speaking, which he evidently enjoys greatly, though it be occasionally trying to his listeners.

"On the afternoon of my second day's drive, the snow, which till then had fallen fine and continuous, ceased, and my Jehu, suddenly interrupting himself in the midst of some exciting wolf story, quite in keeping with the time of year and the wild surroundings, pointed to a distant spot against the grey sky to the north-west, between two wood-covered folds of ground—the first eastern spurs of the great Carpathian chain.

"'There stands Yany,' said he.

"I looked at my far-off goal with interest. As we drew nearer, the sinking sun, just dipping behind the hills, tinged the now distinct frontage with a cold, copperlike gleam, but it was only for a minute; the next the building became nothing more to the eye than a black irregular silhouette against the crimson sky.

"Before we entered the long, steep avenue of poplars, the early winter darkness was upon us, rendered all the more depressing by grey mists which gave a ghostly aspect to such objects as the sheen of the snow rendered visible. Once or twice there were feeble flashes of light looming in iridescent halos as we passed little clusters of hovels, but for which I should have been induced to fancy that the great Hof stood alone in the wilderness, such was the deathly stillness around. But even as the tall square building rose before us above the vapour, yellow lighted in various stories, and mighty in height and breadth, there broke upon my ear a deep-mouthed, menacing bay, which gave at once almost alarming reality to the eerie surroundings.

"'His lordship's boar and wolf hounds,' quoth my charioteer calmly, unmindful of the regular pandemonium of howls and barks which ensued as he skilfully turned his horses through the gateway and flogged the tired beasts into a sort of shambling canter that we might land with glory before the house door; a weakness common, I believe, to drivers of all nations.

"I alighted in the court of honour, and while awaiting an answer to my tug at the bell, stood, broken with fatigue, depressed, chilled and aching, questioning the wisdom of my proceedings and the amount of comfort, physical and moral, that was likely to await me in a *tête-à-tête* visit with a well-mannered savage in his own home.

"The unkempt tribe of stable retainers who began to gather round me and my rough vehicle in the gloom, with their evil-smelling sheepskins and their resigned battered visages, were not calculated to reassure me. Yet when the door opened, there stood a smart chasseur and a solemn major-domo who might but just have stepped out of Mayfair; and there was displayed a spreading vista of warm, deep-coloured halls, with here a statue and there a stuffed bear, and underfoot pile carpets strewn with rarest skins.

"Marvelling, yet comforted withal, I followed the solemn butler, who received me with the deference due to an expected guest and expressed the master's regret for his enforced absence till dinner-time. I traversed vast rooms, each more sumptuous than the last, feeling the strangeness of the contrast between the outer desolation and this sybaritic excess of luxury growing ever more strongly upon me; caught a glimpse of a picture-gallery, where peculiar yet admirably executed latter-day French pictures hung side by side with ferocious boar hunts of Snyder and such kin; and, at length, was ushered into a most cheerful room, modern to excess in its comfortable promise, where, in addition to the tall stove necessary for warmth, there burned on an open hearth a vastly pleasant fire of resinous logs, and where, on a low table, awaited me a dainty service of fragrant Russian tea.

"My impression of utter novelty seemed somehow enhanced by this unexpected refinement in the heart of the solitudes and in such a rugged shell, and yet, when I came to reflect, it was only characteristic of my cosmopolitan host. But another surprise was in store for me.

"When I had recovered bodily warmth and mental equilibrium in my downy armchair, before the roaring logs, and during the delicious absorption of my second glass of tea, I turned my attention to the French valet, evidently the baron's own man, who was deftly unpacking my portmanteau, and who, unless my practised eye deceived me, asked for nothing better than to entertain me with agreeable conversation the while.

"'Your master is out, then,' quoth I, knowing that the most trivial remark would suffice to start him.

"True, monseigneur was out; he was desolated in despair (this with the national amiable and imaginative instinct); but it was doubtless important business. M. le Baron had the visit of his factor during the midday meal; had left the table hurriedly, and had not been seen since. Madame la Baronne had been a little suffering, but she would receive monsieur.

"'Madame!' exclaimed I, astounded. 'Is your master then married? since when?'—visions of a fair Tartar, fit mate for my baron, immediately springing somewhat alluringly before my mental vision. But the answer dispelled the picturesque fancy.

"'Oh yes,' said the man, with a somewhat peculiar expression. 'Yes, monseigneur is married. Did monsieur not know? And yet it was from England that monseigneur brought back his wife.'

"'An Englishwoman!'

"My first thought was one of pity; an Englishwoman alone in this wilderness—two days' drive from even a railway station—and at the mercy of Kossowski! But the next minute I reversed my judgment. Probably she adored her rufous lord, took his veneer of courtesy—a veneer of the most exquisite polish, I grant you, but perilously thin—for the very perfection of chivalry. Or perchance it was his inner savageness itself that charmed her; the most refined women often amaze one by the fascination which the preponderance of the brute in the opposite sex seems to have for them.

"I was anxious to hear more.

"'Is it not dull for the lady here at this time of year?'

"The valet raised his shoulders with a gesture of despair that was almost passionate.

"Dull! Ah, monsieur could not conceive to himself the dulness of it. That poor Madame la Baronne! not even a little child to keep her company on the long, long days when there was nothing but snow in the heaven and on the earth and the howling of the wind and the dogs to cheer her. At the beginning, indeed, it had been different; when the master first brought home his bride the house was gay enough. It was all redecorated and refurnished to receive her (monsieur should have seen it before, a mere *rendezvous-de-chasse*—for the matter of that so were all the country houses in these parts!) Ah, that was the good time! There were visits month after month; parties, sleighing, dancing, trips to St. Petersburg and Vienna. But this year it seemed they were to have nothing but boars and wolves. How madame could stand it—well, it was not for him to speak—and heaving a deep sigh he delicately inserted my white tie round my collar, and with a flourish twisted it into an irreproachable bow beneath my chin.

"I did not think it right to cross-examine the willing talker any further, especially as, despite his last asseveration, there were evidently volumes he still wished to pour forth; but I confess that, as I made my way slowly out of my room along the noiseless length of passage, I was conscious of an unwonted, not to say vulgar, curiosity concerning the woman who had captivated such a man as the Baron Kossowski.

"In a fit of speculative abstraction I must have taken the wrong turning, for I presently found myself in a long, narrow passage I did not remember. I was retracing my steps when there came the sound of rapid footfalls upon stone flags; a little door flew open in the wall close to me, and a small, thick-set man, huddled in the rough sheepskin of the Galician peasant, with a mangy fur cap on his head, nearly ran headlong into my arms. I was about condescendingly to interpellate him in my best Polish when I caught the gleam of an angry yellow eye and noted the bristle of a red beard—Kossowski!

"Amazed, I fell back a step in silence. With a growl, like an uncouth animal disturbed, he drew his filthy cap over his brow with a savage gesture and pursued his way down the corridor at a sort of wild-boar trot

"This first meeting between host and guest was so odd, so incongruous, that it afforded me plenty of food for a fresh line of conjecture as I traced my way back to the picture-gallery, and from thence successfully to the drawing-room, which, as the door was ajar, I could not this time mistake.

"It was large and lofty and dimly lit by shaded lamps; through the rosy gloom I could at first only just make out a slender figure by the hearth; but as I advanced, this was resolved into a singularly graceful woman in clinging, fur-trimmed velvet gown, who, with one hand resting on the high mantelpiece, the other hanging listlessly by her side, stood gazing down at the crumbling wood fire as if in a dream.

"My friends are kind enough to say that I have a catlike tread; I know not how that may be, at any rate the carpet I was walking upon was thick enough to smother a heavier footfall; not until I was quite close to her did my hostess become aware of my presence. Then she started violently and looked over her shoulder at me with dilating eyes. Evidently a nervous creature, I saw the pulse in her throat, strained by her attitude, flutter like a terrified bird.

"The next instant she had stretched out her hand with sweet, English words of welcome, and the face, which I had been comparing in my mind to that of Guide's Cenci, became transformed by the arch and exquisite smile of a Greuse. For more than two years I had had no intercourse with any of my nationality. I could conceive the sound of his native tongue under such circumstances moving a man in a curious, unexpected fashion.

"I babbled some commonplace reply, after which there was silence while we stood opposite each other, she looking at me expectantly. At length, with a sigh checked by a smile and an overtone of sadness in a voice that yet tried to be sprightly:—

"'Am I then so changed, Mr. Marshfield?' she asked. And all at once I knew her: the girl whose nightingale throat had redeemed the desolation of the evenings at Rathdrum, whose sunny beauty had seemed (even to my celebrated, cold-blooded aestheticism) worthy to haunt a man's dreams. Yes, there was the subtle curve of waist, the warm line of throat, the dainty foot, the slender, tip-tilted fingers—witty fingers, as I had classified them—which I now shook like a true Briton, instead of availing myself of the privilege the country gave me, and kissing her slender wrist.

"But she was changed; and I told her so with unconventional frankness, studying her closely as I spoke.

"'I am afraid,' I said gravely, 'that this place does not agree with you.'

"She shrank from my scrutiny with a nervous movement and flushed to the roots of her red-brown hair. Then she answered coldly that I was wrong, that she was in excellent health, but that she could not expect, any more than other people, to preserve perennial youth (I rapidly calculated she might be two-and-twenty), though indeed, with a little forced laugh, it was scarcely flattering to hear one had altered out of all recognition. Then, without allowing me time to reply, she plunged into a general topic of conversation which, as I should have been obtuse indeed not to take the hint, I did my best to keep up.

"But while she talked of Vienna and Warsaw, of her distant neighbours and last year's visitors, it was evident that her mind was elsewhere; her eye wandered, she lost the thread of her discourse; answered me at random, and smiled her piteous smile incongruously.

"However lonely she might be in her solitary splendour, the company of a countryman was evidently no such welcome diversion.

"After a little while she seemed to feel herself that she was lacking in cordiality, and, bringing her absent gaze to bear upon me with a puzzled, strained look:—

"'I fear you will find it very dull,' she said; 'my husband is so wrapped up this winter in his country life and his sport, you are the first visitor we have had. There is nothing but guns and horses here, and you do not care for these things.'

"The door creaked behind us; and the baron entered, in faultless evening dress. Before she turned toward him I was sharp enough to catch again the upleaping of a quick dread in her eyes, not even so much dread perhaps, I thought afterward, as horror—the horror we notice in some animals at the nearing of a beast of prey. It was gone in a second, and she was smiling. But it was a revelation.

"Perhaps he beat her in Russian fashion, and she as an English woman was narrow-minded enough to resent this; or perhaps merely I had the misfortune to arrive during a matrimonial misunderstanding.

"The baron would not give me leisure to reflect; he was so very effusive in his greeting—not a hint of our previous meeting—unlike my hostess, all in all to me; eager to listen, to reply; almost affectionate, full of references to old times and genial allusions. No doubt when he chose he could be the most charming of men; there were moments when, looking at him in his correct attire, hearkening to his cultured voice, marking his quiet smile and restrained gesture, the almost exaggerated politeness of his manner to his wife, whose fingers he had kissed with pretty, old-fashioned gallantry upon his entrance,

I asked myself, could that encounter in the passage have been a dream? could that savage in the sheepskin be my courteous entertainer?

"'Just as I came in, did I hear my wife say there was nothing for you to do in this place?' he said presently to me. Then, turning to her:—

"'You do not seem to know Mr. Marshfield. Wherever he can open his eyes, there is for him something to see which might not interest other men. He will find things in my library which I have no notion of. He will discover objects for scientific observation in all the members of my household, not only in the good-looking maids—though he could, I have no doubt, tell their points as I could those of a horse. We have maidens here of several distinct races, Marshfield. We have also witches, and Jew leeches, and holy daft people. In any case, Yany, with all its dependencies, material, male, and female, are at your disposal, for what you can make out of them.'

"'It is good,' he went on gaily, 'that you should happen to have this happy disposition, for I fear that, no later than to-morrow, I may have to absent myself from home. I have heard that there are news of wolves—they menace to be a greater pest than usual this winter, but I am going to drive them on quite a new plan, and it will go hard with me if I don't come even with them. Well for you, by the way, Marshfield, that you did not pass within their scent to-day.' Then, musingly: 'I should not give much for the life of a traveller who happened to wander in these parts just now.' Here he interrupted himself hastily, and went over to his wife who had sunk back on her chair, livid, seemingly on the point of swooning.

"His gaze was devouring; so might a man look at the woman he adored, in his anxiety.

"'What! faint, Violet, alarmed!' His voice was subdued, yet there was an unmistakable thrill of emotion in it.

"'Pshaw!' thought I to myself, 'the man is a model husband.'

"She clenched her hands, and by sheer force of will seemed to pull herself together. These nervous women have often an unexpected fund of strength.

"'Come, that is well,' said the baron, with a flickering smile; 'Mr. Marshfield will think you but badly acclimatized to Poland if a little wolf-scare can upset you. My dear wife is so soft-hearted,' he went on to me, 'that she is capable of making herself quite ill over the sad fate that might have, but has not, overcome you. Or, perhaps,' he added, in a still gentler voice, 'her fear is that I may expose myself to danger for the public weal.'

"She turned her head away, but I saw her set her teeth as if to choke a sob. The baron chuckled in his throat and seemed to luxuriate in the pleasant thought.

"At this moment folding doors were thrown open, and supper was announced. I offered my arm, she rose and took it in silence. This silence she maintained during the first part of the meal, despite her husband's brilliant conversation and almost uproarious spirits. But, by and by, a bright colour mounted to her cheeks and lustre to her eyes. I suppose you will all think me horribly unpoetical if I add that she drank several glasses of champagne one after the other, a fact which perhaps may account for the change.

"At any rate she spoke and laughed and looked lovely, and I did not wonder that the baron could hardly keep his eyes off her. But—whether it was her wifely anxiety or not—it was evident her mind was not at ease through it all, and I fancied that her brightness was feverish, her merriment slightly hysterical.

"After supper—an exquisite one it was—we adjourned together, in foreign fashion, to the drawing-room; the baron threw himself into a chair and, somewhat with the air of a pasha, demanded music. He was flushed; the veins of his forehead were swollen and stood out like cords; the wine drunk at table was potent; even through my phlegmatic frame it ran hotly.

"She hesitated a moment or two, then docilely sat down to the piano. That she could sing I have already made clear; how she could sing, with what pathos, passion, as well as perfect art, I had never realized before.

"When the song was ended she remained for a while, with eyes lost in distance, very still, save for her quick breathing. It was clear she was moved by the music; indeed she must have thrown her whole soul into it.

"At first we, the audience, paid her the rare compliment of silence. Then the baron broke forth into loud applause.

"'Brava, brava! that was really said *con amore*. A delicious love-song, delicious—but French. You must sing one of our Slav melodies for Marshfield before you allow us to go and smoke.'

"She started from her reverie with a flush, and after a pause struck slowly a few simple chords, then began one of those strangely sweet yet intensely pathetic Russian airs which give one a curious revelation of the profound, endless melancholy lurking in the national mind.

"'What do you think of it?' asked the baron of me when it ceased.

"'What I have always thought of such music—it is that of a hopeless people; poetical, crushed, and resigned.'

"He gave a loud laugh. 'Hear the analyst, the psychologue—why, man, it is a love-song! Is it possible that we, uncivilized, are truer realists than our hyper-cultured Western neighbours? Have we gone to the root of the matter, in our simple way?'

"The baroness got up abruptly. She looked white and spent; there were bistre circles round her eyes.

"'I am tired,' she said, with dry lips. 'You will excuse me, Mr. Marshfield, I must really go to bed.'

"'Go to bed, go to bed,' cried her husband gaily. Then, quoting in Russian from the song she had just sung: 'Sleep, my little soft white dove; my little innocent, tender lamb!'

"She hurried from the room. The baron laughed again, and, taking me familiarly by the arm led me to his own set of apartments for the promised smoke. He ensconced me in an armchair, placed cigars of every description, and a Turkish pipe ready to my hand and a little table on which stood cut glass flasks and beakers in tempting array.

"After I had selected my cigar with some precautions, I glanced at him over a careless remark, and was startled to see a sudden alteration in his whole look and attitude.

"'You will forgive me, Marshfield,' he said, as he caught my eye, speaking with spasmodic politeness. 'It is more than probable that I shall have to set out upon this chase I spoke of to-night, and I must now go and change my clothes, that I may be ready to start at any moment. This is the hour when it is most likely these hell-beasts are to be got at. You have all you want, I hope,' interrupting an outbreak of ferocity by an effort after his former courtesy.

"It was curious to watch the man of the world struggling with the primitive man.

"'But, baron,' said I, 'I do not at all see the fun of sticking at home like this. You know my passion for witnessing everything new, strange, and outlandish. You will surely not refuse me such an opportunity for observation as a midnight wolf-raid. I will do my best not to be in the way if you will take me with you.'

"At first it seemed as if he had some difficulty in realizing the drift of my words, he was so engrossed by some inner thought. But as I repeated them, he gave vent to a loud cachinnation.

"'By heaven! I like your spirit,' he exclaimed, clapping me strongly on the shoulder. 'Of course you shall come. You shall,' he repeated, 'and I promise you a sight, a hunt such as you never heard or dreamt of—you will be able to tell them in England the sort of thing we can do here in that line—such wolves are rare quarry,' he added, looking slyly at me, 'and I have a new plan for getting at them.'"

"There was a long pause, and then there rose in the stillness the unearthly howling of the baron's hounds, a cheerful sound which only their owner's somewhat loud converse of the evening had kept from becoming excessively obtrusive.

"'Hark at them—the beauties!' cried he, showing his short, strong teeth, pointed like a dog's, in a wide grin of anticipative delight. 'They have been kept on pretty short commons, poor things! They are hungry. By the way, Marshfield, you can sit tight to a horse, I trust? If you were to roll off, you know, these splendid fellows they would chop you up in a second. They would chop you up,' he repeated unctuously, 'snap, crunch, gobble, and there would be an end of you!'

"'If I could not ride a decent horse without being thrown,' I retorted, a little stung by his manner, 'after my recent three months' torture with the Guard Cossacks, I should indeed be a hopeless subject. Do not think of frightening me from the exploit, but say frankly if my company would be displeasing.'

"'Tut!' he said, waving his hand impatiently, 'it is your affair. I have warned you. Go and get ready if you want to come. Time presses.'

"I was determined to be of the fray; my blood was up. I have hinted that the baron's Tokay had stirred it.

"I went to my room and hurriedly donned clothes more suitable for rough nightwork. My last care was to slip into my pockets a brace of double-barrelled pistols which formed part of my travelling kit.

"When I returned I found the baron already booted and spurred; this without metaphor. He was stretched full length on the divan, and did not speak as I came in, or even look at me. Chewing an unlit cigar, with eyes fixed on the ceiling, he was evidently following some absorbing train of ideas.

"The silence was profound; time went by; it grew oppressive; at length, wearied out, I fell, over my chibouque, into a doze filled with puzzling visions, out of which I was awakened with a start. My companion had sprung up, very lightly, to his feet. In his throat was an odd, half-suppressed cry, gruesome to hear. He stood on tiptoe, with eyes fixed, as though looking through the wall, and I distinctly saw his ears point in the intensity of his listening.

"After a moment, with hasty, noiseless energy, and without the slightest ceremony, he blew the lamps out, drew back the heavy curtains and threw the tall window wide open.

"A rush of icy air, and the bright rays of the moon—gibbous, I remember, in her third quarter—filled the room. Outside, the mist had condensed, and the view was unrestricted over the white plains at the foot of the hill.

"The baron stood motionless in the open window, callous to the cold in which, after a minute, I could hardly keep my teeth from chattering, his head bent forward, still listening. I listened too, with 'all my ears,' but could not catch a sound; indeed the silence over the great expanse of snow might have been called awful; even the dogs were mute.

"Presently, far, far away, came a faint tinkle of bells; so faint, at first, that I thought it was but fancy, then distincter. It was even more eerie than the silence I thought, though I knew it could come but from some passing sleigh. All at once that ceased, and again my duller senses could perceive nothing, though I saw by my host's craning neck that he was more on the alert than ever. But at last I too heard once more, this time not bells, but as it were the tread of horses muffled by the snow, intermittent and dull yet drawing nearer. And then in the inner silence of the great house it seemed to me I caught the noise of closing doors; but here the hounds, as if suddenly becoming alive to some disturbance, raised the same fearsome concert of yells and barks with which they had greeted my arrival, and listening became useless.

"I had risen to my feet. My host, turning from the windows, seized my shoulder with a fierce grip, and bade me 'hold my noise;' for a second or two I stood motionless under his iron talons, then he released me with an exultant whisper:—

"'Now for our chase!' and made for the door with a spring. Hastily gulping down a mouthful of arrack from one of the bottles on the table, I followed him, and, guided by the sound of his footsteps before me, groped my way through passages black as Erebus.

"After a time, which seemed a long one, a small door was flung open in front, and I saw Kossowski glide into the moonlit courtyard and cross the square. When I too came out he was disappearing into the gaping darkness of the open stable door, and there I overtook him.

"A man who seemed to have been sleeping in a corner jumped up at our entrance, and led out a horse ready saddled. In obedience to a gruff order from his master, as the latter mounted, he then brought forward another which he had evidently thought to ride himself and held the stirrup for me.

"We came delicately forth, and the Cossack hurriedly barred the great door behind us—I caught a glimpse of his worn, scarred face by the moonlight, as he peeped after us for a second before shutting himself in; it was stricken with terror.

"The baron trotted briskly toward the kennels from whence there was now issuing a truly infernal clangour, and, as my steed followed suit of his own accord, I could see how he proceeded dexterously to unbolt the gates without dismounting, while the beasts within dashed themselves against them and tore the ground in their fury of impatience.

"He smiled, as he swung back the barriers at last, and his 'beauties' came forth. Seven or eight monstrous brutes, hounds of a kind unknown to me; fulvous and sleek of coat, tall on their legs, square-headed, long-tailed, deep-chested; with terrible jaws slobbering in eagerness. They leapt around and up at us, much to our horses' distaste. Kossowski, still smiling, lashed at them unsparingly with his hunting whip, and they responded, not with yells of pain, but with snarls of fury.

"Managing his restless steed and his cruel whip with consummate ease, my host drove the unruly crew before him, out of the precincts, then halted and bent down from his saddle to examine some slight prints in the snow which led, not the way I had come, but toward what seemed another avenue. In a second or two the hounds were gathered round this spot, their great snake-like tails quivering, nose to earth, yelping with excitement. I had some ado to manage my horse, and my eyesight was far from being as keen as the baron's, but I had then no doubt he had come already upon wolf-tracks, and I shuddered mentally, thinking of the sleigh-bells.

"Suddenly Kossowski raised himself from his strained position; under his low fur cap his face, with its fixed smile, looked scarcely human in the white light; and then we broke into a hand canter just as the hounds dashed, in a compact body, along the trail.

"But we had not gone more than a few hundred yards before they began to falter, then straggled, stopped, and ran back and about with dismal cries. It was clear to me they had lost the scent. My companion reined in his horse, and mine, luckily a well-trained brute, halted of himself.

"We had reached a bend in a broad avenue of firs and larches, and just where we stood, and where the hounds ever returned and met nose to nose in frantic conclave, the snow was trampled and soiled, and a little further on planed in a great sweep, as if by a turning sleigh. Beyond was a double-furrowed track of skates and regular hoof-prints leading far away.

"Before I had time to reflect upon the bearing of this unexpected interruption, Kossowski, as if suddenly possessed by a devil, fell upon the hounds with his whip, flogging them upon the new track, uttering the while the most savage cries I have ever heard issue from human throat. The disappointed beasts were nothing loth to seize upon another trail; after a second of hesitation they had understood, and were off upon it at a tearing pace, and we after them at the best speed of our horses.

"Some unformed idea that we were going to escort, or rescue, benighted travellers flickered dimly in my mind as I galloped through the night air; but when I managed to approach my companion and called out to him for explanation, he only turned half round and grinned at me.

"Before us lay now the white plain, scintillating under the high moon's rays. That light is deceptive; I could be sure of nothing upon the wide expanse, but of the dark, leaping figures of the hounds already spread out in a straggling line, some right ahead, others just in front of us. In a short time also the icy wind, cutting my face mercilessly as we increased our pace, well-nigh blinded me with tears of cold.

"I can hardly realize how long this pursuit after an unseen prey lasted; I can only remember that I was getting rather faint with fatigue, and ignominiously held on to my pommel, when all of a sudden the black outline of a sleigh merged into sight in front of us.

"I rubbed my smarting eyes with my benumbed hand; we were gaining upon it second by second; two of those hell-hounds of the baron's were already within a few leaps of it.

"Soon I was able to make out two figures, one standing up and urging the horses on with whip and voice, the other clinging to the back seat and looking toward us in an attitude of terror. A great fear crept into my half frozen brain—were we not bringing deadly danger, instead of help to these travellers? Great God! did the baron mean to use them as a bait for his new method of wolf-hunting?

"I would have turned upon Kossowski with a cry of expostulation or warning, but he, urging on his hounds, as he galloped on their flank, howling and gesticulating like a veritable Hun, passed me by like a flash, and all at once I knew."

Marshfield paused for a moment and sent his pale smile round upon his listeners, who now showed no signs of sleepiness; he knocked the ash from his cigar, twisted the latter round in his mouth, and added dryly:—

"And I confess it seemed to me a little strong, even for a baron in the Carpathians. The travellers were our quarry. But the reason why the Lord of Yany had turned man-hunter I was yet to learn. Just then I had to direct my energies to frustrating his plans. I used my spurs mercilessly. Whilst I drew up even with him I saw the two figures in the sleigh change places; he who had hitherto driven now faced back, while his companion took the reins; there was the pale blue sheen of a revolver barrel under the moonlight, followed by a yellow flash, and the nearest hound rolled over in the snow.

"With an oath the baron twisted round in his saddle to call up and urge on the remainder. My horse had taken fright at the report and dashed irresistibly forward, bringing me at once almost level with the fugitives, and the next instant the revolver was turned menacingly toward me. There was no time to explain; my pistol was already drawn, and as another of the brutes bounded up, almost under my horse's feet, I loosed it upon him—I must have let off both barrels at once, for the weapon flew out of my hand, but the hound's back was broken. I presume the traveller understood; at any rate he did not fire at me.

"In moments of intense excitement like these, strangely enough, the mind is extraordinarily open to impressions. I shall never forget that man's countenance, in the sledge, as he stood upright and defied us in his mortal danger; it was young, very handsome, the features not distorted, but set into a sort of desperate, stony calm, and I knew it, beyond all doubt, for that of an Englishman. And then I saw his companion—it was the baron's wife.

"It takes a long time to say all this; it only required an instant to see it. The loud explosion of my pistol had hardly ceased to ring before the baron, with a fearful imprecation, was upon me. First he lashed at me with his whip as we tore along side by side, and then I saw him wind the reins round his off-arm and bend over, and I felt his angry fingers close tightly on my right foot. The next instant I should have been lifted out of my saddle, but there came another shot from the sledge. The baron's horse plunged and stumbled, and the baron, hanging on to my foot with a fierce grip, was wrenched from his seat. His horse, however, was up again immediately, and I was released, and then I caught a confused glimpse of the frightened and wounded animal galloping wildly away to the right, leaving a black track of blood behind him in the snow, his master, entangled in the reins, running with incredible swiftness by his side and endeavouring to vault back into the saddle.

"And now came to pass a terrible thing which, in his savage plans, my host had doubtless never anticipated.

"One of the hounds that had during this short check recovered lost ground, coming across this hot trail of blood, turned away from his course, and with a joyous yell darted after the running man. In another instant the remainder of the pack were upon the new scent.

"As soon as I could stop my horse, I tried to turn him in the direction the new chase had taken, but just then, through the night air, over the receding sound of the horse's scamper and the sobbing of the pack in full cry, there came a long scream, and after that a sickening silence. And I knew that somewhere yonder, under the beautiful moonlight, the Baron Kossowski was being devoured by his starving dogs.

"I looked round, with the sweat on my face, vaguely, for some human being to share the horror of the moment, and I saw, gliding away, far away, in the white distance, the black silhouette of the sledge."

"Well?" said we, in divers tones of impatience, curiosity, or horror, according to our divers temperaments, as the speaker uncrossed his legs and gazed at us in mild triumph, with all the air of having said his say, and satisfactorily proved his point.

"Well," repeated he, "what more do you want to know? It will interest you but slightly, I am sure, to hear how I found my way back to the Hof; or how I told as much as I deemed prudent of the evening's gruesome work to the baron's servants, who, by the way, to my amazement, displayed the profoundest and most unmistakable sorrow at the tidings, and sallied forth (at their head the Cossack who had seen us depart) to seek for his remains. Excuse the unpleasantness of the remark; I fear the dogs must have left very little of him; he had dieted them so carefully. However, since it was to have been a case of 'chop, crunch, and gobble,' as the baron had it, I preferred that that particular fate should have overtaken him than me—or, for that matter, either of these two country people of ours in the sledge.

"Nor am I going to inflict upon you," continued Marshfield, after draining his glass, "a full account of my impressions when I found myself once more in that immense, deserted, and stricken house, so luxuriously prepared for the mistress who had fled from it; how I philosophized over all this, according to my wont; the conjectures I made as to the first acts of the drama, the untold sufferings my country-woman must have endured from the moment her husband first grew jealous till she determined on this desperate step; as to how and when she had met her lover, how they communicated, and how the baron had discovered the intended flitting in time to concoct his characteristic revenge.

"One thing you may be sure of, I had no mind to remain at Yany an hour longer than necessary. I even contrived to get well clear of the neighbourhood before the lady's absence was discovered. Luckily for me—or I might have been taxed with connivance; though indeed the simple household did not seem to know what suspicion was, and accepted my account with childlike credence—very typical, and very convenient to me at the same time."

"But how do you know," said one of us, "that the man was her lover?—he might have been her brother or some other relative?"

"That," said Marshfield, with his little flat laugh, "I happen to have ascertained—and, curiously enough, only a few weeks ago. It was at the play, between the acts, from my comfortable seat (first row of the pit), I was looking leisurely round the house when I caught sight of a woman, in a box, close by, whose head was turned from me, and who presented the somewhat unusual spectacle of a young neck and shoulders of the most exquisite contour—and perfectly gray hair; and not dull gray, but rather of a pleasing tint—like frosted silver. This aroused my curiosity. I brought my glasses to a focus on her, and waited patiently till she turned round. Then I recognized the Baroness Kossowski, and I no longer wondered at the young hair being white.

"Yet she looked placid and happy; strangely so, it seemed to me, under the sudden reviving in my memory of such scenes as I have now described. But presently I understood further; beside her, in close attendance, was the man of the sledge, a handsome fellow, with much of a military air about him.

"During the course of the evening, as I watched, I saw a friend of mine come into the box, and at the end I slipped out into the passage to catch him as he came out.

"'Who is the woman with the white hair?' I asked. Then, in the fragmentary style approved of by ultra-fashionable young men—this earnest-languid mode of speech presents curious similarities in all languages—he told me: 'Most charming couple in London—awfully pretty, wasn't she? *He* had been in the Guards—*attaché* at Vienna once—they adored each other. White hair, devilish queer, wasn't it? Suited her, somehow. And then she had been married to a Russian, or something, somewhere in the wilds, and their names were—' But do you know," said Marshfield, interrupting himself, "I think I had better let you find that out for yourselves, if you care."

II

A MAN AND SOME OTHERS

STEPHEN CRANE

I

Dark mesquit spread from horizon to horizon. There was no house or horseman from which a mind could evolve a city or a crowd. The world was declared to be a desert and unpeopled. Sometimes, however, on days when no heat-mist arose, a blue shape, dun, of the substance of a specter's veil, appeared in the southwest, and a pondering sheep-herder might remember that there were mountains.

In the silence of these plains the sudden and childish banging of a tin pan could have made an iron-nerved man leap into the air. The sky was ever flawless; the manoeuvring of clouds was an unknown pageant; but at times a sheep-herder could see, miles away, the long, white streamers of dust rising from the feet of another's flock, and the interest became intense.

Bill was arduously cooking his dinner, bending over the fire and toiling like a blacksmith. A movement, a flash of strange colour, perhaps, off in the bushes, caused him suddenly to turn his head. Presently he arose, and, shading his eyes with his hand, stood motionless and gazing. He perceived at last a Mexican sheep-herder winding through the brush toward his camp.

"Hello!" shouted Bill.

The Mexican made no answer, but came steadily forward until he was within some twenty yards. There he paused, and, folding his arms, drew himself up in the manner affected by the villain in the play. His serape muffled the lower part of his face, and his great sombrero shaded his brow. Being unexpected and also silent, he had something of the quality of an apparition; moreover, it was clearly his intention to be mystic and sinister.

The American's pipe, sticking carelessly in the corner of his mouth, was twisted until the wrong side was uppermost, and he held his frying-pan poised in the air. He surveyed with evident surprise this apparition in the mesquit. "Hell, José!" he said; "what's the matter?"

The Mexican spoke with the solemnity of funeral tellings: "Beel, you mus' geet off range. We want you geet off range. We no like. Un'erstan'? We no like."

"What you talking about?" said Bill. "No like what?"

"We no like you here. Un'erstan'? Too mooch. You mus' geet out. We no like. Un'erstan'?"

"Understand? No: I don't know what the blazes you're gittin' at." Bill's eyes wavered in bewilderment, and his jaw fell. "I must git out? I must git off the range? What you givin' us?"

The Mexican unfolded his serape with his small yellow hand. Upon his face was then to be seen a smile that was gently, almost caressingly, murderous. "Beel," he said, "git out!"

Bill's arm dropped until the frying-pan was at his knee. Finally he turned again toward the fire. "Go on, you dog-gone little yaller rat!" he said over his shoulder. "You fellers can't chase me off this range. I got as much right here as anybody."

"Beel," answered the other in a vibrant tone, thrusting his head forward and moving one foot, "you geet out or we keel you."

"Who will?" said Bill.

"I—and the others." The Mexican tapped his breast gracefully.

Bill reflected for a time, and then he said: "You ain't got no manner of license to warn me off'n this range, and I won't move a rod. Understand? I've got rights, and I suppose if I don't see 'em through, no one is likely to give me a good hand and help me lick you fellers, since I'm the only white man in half a day's ride. Now, look: if you fellers try to rush this camp, I'm goin' to plug about fifty per cent. of the gentlemen present, sure. I'm goin' in fur trouble, an' I'll git a lot of you. 'Nuther thing: if I was a fine valuable caballero like you, I'd stay in the rear till the shootin' was done, because I'm goin' to make a particular p'int of shootin' you through the chest." He grinned affably, and made a gesture of dismissal.

As for the Mexican, he waved his hands in a consummate expression of indifference. "Oh, all right," he said. Then, in a tone of deep menace and glee, he added: "We will keel you eef you no geet. They have decide."

"They have, have they?" said Bill. "Well, you tell them to go to the devil!"

II

As his Mexican friend tripped blithely away, Bill turned with a thoughtful face to his frying-pan and his fire. After dinner he drew his revolver from its scarred old holster, and examined every part of it. It was the revolver that had dealt death to the foreman, and it had also been in free fights in which it had dealt death to several or none. Bill loved it because its allegiance was more than that of man, horse, or dog. It questioned neither social nor moral position; it obeyed alike the saint and the assassin. It was the claw of the eagle, the tooth of the lion, the poison of the snake; and when he swept it from its holster, this minion smote where he listed, even to the battering of a far penny. Wherefore it was his dearest possession, and was not to be exchanged in southwestern Texas for a handful of rubies.

During the afternoon he moved through his monotony of work and leisure with the same air of deep meditation. The smoke of his supper time fire was curling across the shadowy sea of mesquit when the instinct of the plainsman warned him that the stillness, the desolation, was again invaded. He saw a motionless horseman in black outline against the pallid sky. The silhouette displayed serape and sombrero, and even the Mexican spurs as large as pies. When this black figure began to move toward the camp, Bill's hand dropped to his revolver.

The horseman approached until Bill was enabled to see pronounced American features, and a skin too red to grow on a Mexican face. Bill released his grip on his revolver.

"Hello!" called the horseman.

"Hello!" answered Bill.

The horseman cantered forward. "Good evening," he said, as he again drew rein.

"Good evenin'," answered Bill, without committing himself by too much courtesy.

For a moment the two men scanned each other in a way that is not ill-mannered on the plains, where one is in danger of meeting horse-thieves or tourists.

Bill saw a type which did not belong in the mesquit. The young fellow had invested in some Mexican trappings of an expensive kind. Bill's eyes searched the outfit for some sign of craft, but there was none. Even with his local regalia, it was clear that the young man was of a far, black northern city. He had discarded the enormous stirrups of his Mexican saddle; he used the small English stirrup, and his feet were thrust forward until the steel tightly gripped his ankles. As Bill's eyes travelled over the stranger, they lighted suddenly upon the stirrups and the thrust feet, and immediately he smiled in a friendly way. No dark purpose could dwell in the innocent heart of a man who rode thus on the plains.

As for the stranger, he saw a tattered individual with a tangle of hair and beard, and with a complexion turned brick-colour from the sun and whiskey. He saw a pair of eyes that at first looked at him as the wolf looks at the wolf, and then became childlike, almost timid, in their glance. Here was evidently a man who had often stormed the iron walls of the city of success, and who now sometimes valued himself as the rabbit values his prowess.

The stranger smiled genially, and sprang from his horse. "Well, sir, I suppose you will let me camp here with you to-night?"

"Eh?" said Bill.

"I suppose you will let me camp here with you to-night?"

Bill for a time seemed too astonished for words.

"Well," he answered, scowling in inhospitable annoyance, "well, I don't believe this here is a good place to camp to-night, Mister."

The stranger turned quickly from his saddle-girth.

"What?" he said in surprise. "You don't want me here? You don't want me to camp here?"

Bill's feet scuffled awkwardly, and he looked steadily at a cactus-plant. "Well, you see, Mister," he said, "I'd like your company well enough, but—you see, some of these here greasers are goin' to chase me off the range to-night; and while I might like a man's company all right, I couldn't let him in for no such game when he ain't got nothin' to do with the trouble."

"Going to chase you off the range?" cried the stranger.

"Well, they said they were goin' to do it," said Bill.

"And—great heavens!—will they kill you, do you think?"

"Don't know. Can't tell till afterward. You see, they take some feller that's alone like me, and then they rush his camp when he ain't quite ready for 'em, and ginerally plug 'im with a sawed-off shot-gun load before he has a chance to git at 'em. They lay around and wait for their chance, and it comes soon enough. Of course a feller alone like me has got to let up watching some time. Maybe they ketch 'im asleep. Maybe the feller gits tired waiting, and goes out in broad day, and kills two or three just to make the whole crowd pile on him and settle the thing. I heard of a case like that once. It's awful hard on a man's mind—to git a gang after him."

"And so they're going to rush your camp tonight?" cried the stranger. "How do you know? Who told you?"

"Feller come and told me."

"And what are you going to do? Fight?"

"Don't see nothin' else to do," answered Bill, gloomily, still staring at the cactus-plant.

There was a silence. Finally the stranger burst out in an amazed cry. "Well, I never heard of such a thing in my life! How many of them are there?"

"Eight," answered Bill. "And now look-a-here; you ain't got no manner of business foolin' around here just now, and you might better lope off before dark. I don't ask no help in this here row. I know your happening along here just now don't give me no call on you, and you'd better hit the trail."

"Well, why in the name of wonder don't you go get the sheriff?" cried the stranger.

"Oh, hell!" said Bill.

III

Long, smouldering clouds spread in the western sky, and to the east silver mists lay on the purple gloom of the wilderness.

Finally, when the great moon climbed the heavens and cast its ghastly radiance upon the bushes, it made a new and more brilliant crimson of the campfire, where the flames capered merrily through its mesquit branches, filling the silence with the fire chorus, an ancient melody which surely bears a message of the inconsequence of individual tragedy—a message that is in the boom of the sea, the shiver of the wind through the grass-blades, the silken clash of hemlock boughs.

No figures moved in the rosy space of the camp, and the search of the moonbeams failed to disclose a living thing in the bushes. There was no owl-faced clock to chant the weariness of the long silence that brooded upon the plain.

The dew gave the darkness under the mesquit a velvet quality that made air seem nearer to water, and no eye could have seen through it the black things that moved like monster lizards toward the camp. The branches, the leaves, that are fain to cry out when death approaches in the wilds, were frustrated by these mystic bodies gliding with the finesse of the escaping serpent. They crept forward to the last point where assuredly no frantic attempt of the fire could discover them, and there they paused to locate the prey. A romance relates the tale of the black cell hidden deep in the earth, where, upon entering, one sees only the little eyes of snakes fixing him in menaces. If a man could have approached a certain spot in the bushes, he would not have found it romantically necessary to have his hair rise. There would have been sufficient expression of horror in the feeling of the death-hand at the nape of his neck and in his rubber knee-joints.

Two of the bodies finally moved toward each other until for each there grew out of the darkness a face placidly smiling with tender dreams of assassination. "The fool is asleep by the fire, God be praised!" The lips of the other widened in a grin of affectionate appreciation of the fool and his plight. There was some signalling in the gloom and then began a series of subtle rustlings, interjected often with pauses, during which no sound arose but the sound of faint breathing.

A bush stood like a rock in the stream of firelight, sending its long shadow backward. With painful caution the little company travelled along this shadow, and finally arrived at the rear of the bush. Through its branches they surveyed for a moment of comfortable satisfaction a form in a gray blanket extended on the ground near the fire. The smile of joyful anticipation fled quickly, to give place to a quiet air of business. Two men lifted shot-guns with much of the barrels gone, and sighting these weapons through the branches, pulled trigger together.

The noise of the explosions roared over the lonely mesquit as if these guns wished to inform the entire world; and as the grey smoke fled, the dodging company back of the bush saw the blanketed form twitching. Whereupon they burst out in chorus in a laugh, and arose as merry as a lot of banqueters. They gleefully gestured congratulations, and strode bravely into the light of the fire.

Then suddenly a new laugh rang from some unknown spot in the darkness. It was a fearsome laugh of ridicule, hatred, ferocity. It might have been demoniac. It smote them motionless in their gleeful prowl, as the stern voice from the sky smites the legendary malefactor. They might have been a weird group in wax, the light of the dying fire on their yellow faces, and shining athwart their eyes turned toward the darkness whence might come the unknown and the terrible.

The thing in the grey blanket no longer twitched; but if the knives in their hands had been thrust toward it, each knife was now drawn back, and its owner's elbow was thrown upward, as if he expected death from the clouds.

This laugh had so chained their reason that for a moment they had no wit to flee. They were prisoners to their terror. Then suddenly the belated decision arrived, and with bubbling cries they turned to run; but at that instant there was a long flash of red in the darkness, and with the report one of the men shouted a bitter shout, spun once, and tumbled headlong. The thick bushes failed to impede the route of the others.

The silence returned to the wilderness. The tired flames faintly illumined the blanketed thing and the flung corpse of the marauder, and sang the fire chorus, the ancient melody which bears the message of the inconsequence of human tragedy.

IV

"Now you are worse off than ever," said the young man, dry-voiced and awed.

"No, I ain't," said Bill, rebelliously. "I'm one ahead."

After reflection, the stranger remarked, "Well, there's seven more."

They were cautiously and slowly approaching the camp. The sun was flaring its first warming rays over the gray wilderness. Upreared twigs, prominent branches, shone with golden light, while the shadows under the mesquit were heavily blue.

Suddenly the stranger uttered a frightened cry. He had arrived at a point whence he had, through openings in the thicket, a clear view of a dead face.

"Gosh!" said Bill, who at the next instant had seen the thing; "I thought at first it was that there José. That would have been queer, after what I told 'im yesterday."

They continued their way, the stranger wincing in his walk, and Bill exhibiting considerable curiosity.

The yellow beams of the new sun were touching the grim hues of the dead Mexican's face, and creating there an inhuman effect, which made his countenance more like a mask of dulled brass. One hand, grown curiously thinner, had been flung out regardlessly to a cactus bush.

Bill walked forward and stood looking respectfully at the body. "I know that feller; his name is Miguel. He——"

The stranger's nerves might have been in that condition when there is no backbone to the body, only a long groove. "Good heavens!" he exclaimed, much agitated; "don't speak that way!"

"What way?" said Bill. "I only said his name was Miguel."

After a pause the stranger said:

"Oh, I know; but—" He waved his hand. "Lower your voice, or something. I don't know. This part of the business rattles me, don't you see?"

"Oh, all right," replied Bill, bowing to the other's mysterious mood. But in a moment he burst out violently and loud in the most extraordinary profanity, the oaths winging from him as the sparks go from the funnel.

He had been examining the contents of the bundled gray blanket, and he had brought forth, among other things, his frying-pan. It was now only a rim with a handle; the Mexican volley had centred upon it. A Mexican shot-gun of the abbreviated description is ordinarily loaded with flatirons, stove-lids, lead pipe, old horseshoes, sections of chain, window weights, railroad sleepers and spikes, dumbbells, and any other junk which may be at hand. When one of these loads encounters a man vitally, it is likely to make an impression upon him, and a cooking-utensil may be supposed to subside before such an assault of curiosities.

Bill held high his desecrated frying-pan, turning it this way and that way. He swore until he happened to note the absence of the stranger. A moment later he saw him leading his horse from the bushes. In silence and sullenly the young man went about saddling the animal. Bill said, "Well, goin' to pull out?"

The stranger's hands fumbled uncertainly at the throat-latch. Once he exclaimed irritably, blaming the buckle for the trembling of his fingers. Once he turned to look at the dead face with the light of the morning sun upon it. At last he cried, "Oh, I know the whole thing was all square enough—couldn't be squarer—but—somehow or other, that man there takes the heart out of me." He turned his troubled face for another look. "He seems to be all the time calling me a—he makes me feel like a murderer."

"But," said Bill, puzzling, "you didn't shoot him, Mister; I shot him."

"I know; but I feel that way, somehow. I can't get rid of it."

Bill considered for a time; then he said diffidently, "Mister, you'r a' eddycated man, ain't you?"

"What?"

"You're what they call a'—a' eddycated man, ain't you?"

The young man, perplexed, evidently had a question upon his lips, when there was a roar of guns, bright flashes, and in the air such hooting and whistling as would come from a swift flock of steamboilers. The stranger's horse gave a mighty, convulsive spring, snorting wildly in its sudden anguish, fell upon its knees, scrambled afoot again, and was away in the uncanny death-run known to men who have seen the finish of brave horses.

"This comes from discussin' things," cried Bill, angrily.

He had thrown himself flat on the ground facing the thicket whence had come the firing. He could see the smoke winding over the bush-tops. He lifted his revolver, and the weapon came slowly up from the ground and poised like the glittering crest of a snake. Somewhere on his face there was a kind of smile, cynical, wicked, deadly, of a ferocity which at the same time had brought a deep flush to his face, and had caused two upright lines to glow in his eyes.

"Hello, José!" he called, amiable for satire's sake. "Got your old blunderbusses loaded up again yet?"

The stillness had returned to the plain. The sun's brilliant rays swept over the sea of mesquit, painting the far mists of the west with faint rosy light, and high in the air some great bird fled toward the south.

"You come out here," called Bill, again addressing the landscape, "and I'll give you some shootin' lessons. That ain't the way to shoot." Receiving no reply, he began to invent epithets and yell them at the thicket. He was something of a master of insult, and, moreover, he dived into his memory to bring forth imprecations tarnished with age, unused since fluent Bowery days. The occupation amused him, and sometimes he laughed so that it was uncomfortable for his chest to be against the ground.

Finally the stranger, prostrate near him, said wearily, "Oh, they've gone."

"Don't you believe it," replied Bill, sobering swiftly. "They're there yet—every man of 'em."

"How do you know?"

"Because I do. They won't shake us so soon. Don't put your head up, or they'll get you, sure."

Bill's eyes, meanwhile, had not wavered from their scrutiny of the thicket in front. "They're there, all right; don't you forget it. Now you listen." So he called out: "José! Ojo, José! Speak up, *hombre*! I want have talk. Speak up, you yaller cuss, you!"

Whereupon a mocking voice from off in the bushes said, "Senor?"

"There," said Bill to his ally; "didn't I tell you? The whole batch." Again he lifted his voice. "José—look—ain't you gittin' kinder tired? You better go home, you fellers, and git some rest."

The answer was a sudden furious chatter of Spanish, eloquent with hatred, calling down upon Bill all the calamities which life holds. It was as if some one had suddenly enraged a cageful of wildcats. The spirits of all the revenges which they had imagined were loosened at this time, and filled the air.

"They're in a holler," said Bill, chuckling, "or there'd be shootin'."

Presently he began to grow angry. His hidden enemies called him nine kinds of coward, a man who could fight only in the dark, a baby who would run from the shadows of such noble Mexican gentlemen, a dog that sneaked. They described the affair of the previous night, and informed him of the base advantage he had taken of their friend. In fact, they in all sincerity endowed him with every quality which he no less earnestly believed them to possess. One could have seen the phrases bite him as he lay there on the ground fingering his revolver.

V

It is sometimes taught that men do the furious and desperate thing from an emotion that is as even and placid as the thoughts of a village clergyman on Sunday afternoon. Usually, however, it is to be believed that a panther is at the time born in the heart, and that the subject does not resemble a man picking mulberries.

"B' G—!" said Bill, speaking as from a throat filled with dust, "I'll go after 'em in a minute."

"Don't you budge an inch!" cried the stranger, sternly. "Don't you budge!"

"Well," said Bill, glaring at the bushes—"well."

"Put your head down!" suddenly screamed the stranger, in white alarm. As the guns roared, Bill uttered a loud grunt, and for a moment leaned panting on his elbow, while his arm shook like a twig. Then he upreared like a great and bloody spirit of vengeance, his face lighted with the blaze of his last passion. The Mexicans came swiftly and in silence.

The lightning action of the next few moments was of the fabric of dreams to the stranger. The muscular struggle may not be real to the drowning man. His mind may be fixed on the far, straight shadows back of the stars, and the terror of them. And so the fight, and his part in it, had to the stranger only the quality of a picture half drawn. The rush of feet, the spatter of shots, the cries, the swollen faces seen like masks on the smoke, resembled a happening of the night.

And yet afterward certain lines, forms, lived out so strongly from the incoherence that they were always in his memory.

He killed a man, and the thought went swiftly by him, like a feather on a gale, that it was easy to kill a man.

Moreover, he suddenly felt for Bill, this grimy sheep-herder, some deep form of idolatry. Bill was dying, and the dignity of last defeat, this superiority of him who stands in his grave, was in the pose of the lost sheep-herder.

The stranger sat on the ground idly mopping the sweat and powder-stain from his brow. He wore the gentle idiotic smile of an aged beggar as he watched three Mexicans limping and staggering in the distance. He noted at this time that one who still possessed a serape had from it none of the grandeur of the cloaked Spaniard, but that against the sky the silhouette resembled a cornucopia of childhood's Christmas.

They turned to look at him, and he lifted his weary arm to menace them with his revolver. They stood for a moment banded together, and hooted curses at him.

Finally he arose, and, walking some paces, stooped to loosen Bill's gray hands from a throat. Swaying as if slightly drunk, he stood looking down into the still face.

Struck suddenly with a thought, he went about with dulled eyes on the ground, until he plucked his gaudy blanket from where it lay dirty from trampling feet. He dusted it carefully, and then returned and laid it over Bill's form. There he again stood motionless, his mouth just agape and the same stupid glance in his eyes, when all at once he made a gesture of fright and looked wildly about him.

He had almost reached the thicket when he stopped, smitten with alarm. A body contorted, with one arm stiff in the air, lay in his path. Slowly and warily he moved around it, and in a moment the bushes nodding and whispering, their leaf-faces turned toward the scene behind him, swung and swung again into stillness and the peace of the wilderness.

III

THE OUTLAWS

SELMA LAGERLÖF

A peasant who had murdered a monk took to the woods and was made an outlaw. He found there before him in the wilderness another outlaw, a fisherman from the outer-most islands, who had been accused of stealing a herring net. They joined together, lived in a cave, set snares, sharpened darts, baked bread on a granite rock and guarded one another's lives. The peasant never left the woods, but the fisherman, who had not committed such an abominable crime, sometimes loaded game on his shoulders and stole down among men. There he got in exchange for black-cocks, and long-eared hares and fine-limbed red deer, milk and butter, arrow-heads and clothes. These helped the outlaws to sustain life.

The cave where they lived was dug in the side of a hill. Broad stones and thorny-sloe-bushes hid the entrance. Above it stood a thick growing pine-tree. At its roots was the vent-hole of the cave. The rising smoke filtered through the tree's thick branches and vanished into space. The men used to go to and from their dwelling-place, wading in the mountain stream, which ran down the hill. No one looked for their tracks under the merry, bubbling water.

At first they were hunted like wild beasts. The peasants gathered as if for a chase of bear or wolf. The wood was surrounded by men with bows and arrows. Men with spears went through it and left no dark crevice, no bushy thicket unexplored. While the noisy battue hunted through the wood, the outlaws lay in their dark hole, listening breathlessly, panting with terror. The fisherman held out a whole day, but he who had murdered was driven by unbearable fear out into the open, where he could see his enemy. He was seen and hunted, but it seemed to him seven times better than to lie still in helpless inactivity. He fled from his pursuers, slid down precipices, sprang over streams, climbed up perpendicular mountain walls. All latent strength and dexterity in him was called forth by the excitement of danger. His body became elastic like a steel spring, his foot made no false step, his hand never lost its hold, eye and ear were twice as sharp as usual. He understood what the leaves whispered and the rocks warned. When he had climbed up a precipice, he turned toward his pursuers, sending them gibes in biting rhyme. When the whistling darts whizzed by him, he caught them, swift as lightning, and hurled them down on his enemies. As he forced his way through whipping branches, something within him sang a song of triumph.

The bald mountain ridge ran through the wood and alone on its summit stood a lofty fir. The red-brown trunk was bare, but in the branching top rocked an eagle's nest. The fugitive was now so audaciously bold that he climbed up there, while his pursuers looked for him on the wooded slopes. There he sat twisting the young eaglets' necks, while the hunt passed by far below him. The male and female eagle, longing for revenge, swooped down on the ravisher. They fluttered before his face, they struck with their beaks at his eyes, they beat him with their wings and tore with their claws bleeding weals in his weather-beaten skin. Laughing, he fought with them. Standing upright in the shaking nest, he cut at them with his sharp knife and forgot in the pleasure of the play his danger and his pursuers. When he found time to look for them, they had gone by to some other part of the forest. No one had thought to look for their prey on the bald mountain-ridge. No one had raised his eyes to the clouds to see him practising boyish tricks and sleep-walking feats while his life was in the greatest danger.

The man trembled when he found that he was saved. With shaking hands he caught at a support, giddy he measured the height to which he had climbed. And moaning with the fear of falling, afraid of the birds, afraid of being seen, afraid of everything, he slid down the trunk. He laid himself down on the ground, so as not to be seen, and dragged himself forward over the rocks until the underbrush covered him. There he hid himself under the young pine-tree's tangled branches. Weak and powerless, he sank down on the moss. A single man could have captured him.

* * * * *

Tord was the fisherman's name. He was not more than sixteen years old, but strong and bold. He had already lived a year in the woods.

The peasant's name was Berg, with the surname Rese. He was the tallest and the strongest man in the whole district, and moreover handsome and well-built. He was broad in the shoulders and slender in the waist. His hands were as well shaped as if he had never done any hard work. His hair was brown and his skin fair. After he had been some time in the woods he acquired in all ways a more formidable appearance. His eyes became piercing, his eyebrows grew bushy, and the muscles which knitted them lay finger thick above his nose. It showed now more plainly than before how the upper part of his athlete's brow projected over the lower. His lips closed more firmly than of old, his whole face was thinner, the hollows at the temples grew very deep, and his powerful jaw was much more prominent. His body was less well filled out but his muscles were as hard as steel. His hair grew suddenly grey.

Young Tord could never weary of looking at this man. He had never before seen anything so beautiful and powerful. In his imagination he stood high as the forest, strong as the sea. He served him as a master and worshipped him as a god. It was a matter of course that Tord should carry the hunting spears, drag home the game, fetch the water and build the fire. Berg Rese accepted all his services, but almost never gave him a friendly word. He despised him because he was a thief.

The outlaws did not lead a robber's or brigand's life: they supported themselves by hunting and fishing. If Berg Rese had not murdered a holy man, the peasants would soon have ceased to pursue him and have left him in peace in the mountains. But they feared great disaster to the district, because he who had raised his hand against the servant of God was still unpunished. When Tord came down to the valley with game, they offered him riches and pardon for his own crime if he would show them the way to Berg Rese's hole, so that they might take him while he slept. But the boy had always refused; and if anyone tried to sneak after him up to the wood, he led him so cleverly astray that he gave up the pursuit.

Once Berg asked him if the peasants had not tried to tempt him to betray him, and when he heard what they offered him as a reward, he said scornfully that Tord had been foolish not to accept such a proposal.

Then Tord looked at him with a glance, the like of which Berg Rese had never before seen. Never had any beautiful woman in his youth, never had his wife or child looked so at him. "You are my lord, my elected master," said the glance. "Know that you may strike me and abuse me as you will, I am faithful notwithstanding."

After that Berg Rese paid more attention to the boy and noticed that he was bold to act but timid to speak. He had no fear of death. When the ponds were first frozen, or when the bogs were most dangerous in the spring, when the quagmires were hidden under richly flowering grasses and cloudberry, he took his way over them by choice. He seemed to feel the need of exposing himself to danger as a compensation for the storms and terrors of the ocean, which he had no longer to meet. At night he was afraid in the woods, and even in the middle of the day the darkest thickets or the wide-stretching roots of a fallen pine could frighten him. But when Berg Rese asked him about it, he was too shy even to answer.

Tord did not sleep near the fire, far in in the cave, on the bed which was made soft with moss and warm with skins, but every night, when Berg had fallen asleep, he crept out to the entrance and lay there on a rock. Berg discovered this, and although he well understood the reason, he asked what it meant. Tord would not explain. To escape any more questions, he did not lie at the door for two nights, but then he returned to his post.

One night, when the drifting snow whirled about the forest tops and drove into the thickest underbrush, the driving snowflakes found their way into the outlaws' cave. Tord, who lay just inside the entrance, was, when he waked in the morning, covered by a melting snowdrift. A few days later he fell ill. His lungs wheezed, and when they were expanded to take in air, he felt excruciating pain. He kept up as long as his strength held out, but when one evening he leaned down to blow the fire, he fell over and remained lying.

Berg Rese came to him and told him to go to his bed. Tord moaned with pain and could not raise himself. Berg then thrust his arms under him and carried him there. But he felt as if he had got hold of a slimy snake; he had a taste in the mouth as if he had eaten the unholy horseflesh, it was so odious to him to touch the miserable thief.

He laid his own big bearskin over him and gave him water, more he could not do. Nor was it anything dangerous. Tord was soon well again. But through Berg's being obliged to do his tasks and to be his servant, they had come nearer to one another. Tord dared to talk to him when he sat in the cave in the evening and cut arrow shafts.

"You are of a good race, Berg," said Tord. "Your kinsmen are the richest in the valley. Your ancestors have served with kings and fought in their castles."

"They have often fought with bands of rebels and done the kings great injury," replied Berg Rese.

"Your ancestors gave great feasts at Christmas, and so did you, when you were at home. Hundreds of men and women could find a place to sit in your big house, which was already built before Saint Olof first gave the baptism here in Viken. You owned old silver vessels and great drinking-horns, which passed from man to man, filled with mead."

Again Berg Rese had to look at the boy. He sat up with his legs hanging out of the bed and his head resting on his hands, with which he at the same time held back the wild masses of hair which would fall over his eyes. His face had become pale and delicate from the ravages of sickness. In his eyes fever still burned. He smiled at the pictures he conjured up: at the adorned house, at the silver vessels, at the guests in gala array and at Berg Rese, sitting in the seat of honour in the hall of his ancestors. The peasant thought that no one had ever looked at him with such shining, admiring eyes, or thought him so magnificent, arrayed in his festival clothes, as that boy thought him in the torn skin dress.

He was both touched and provoked. That miserable thief had no right to admire him.

"Were there no feasts in your house?" he asked.

Tord laughed. "Out there on the rocks with father and mother! Father is a wrecker and mother is a witch. No one will come to us."

"Is your mother a witch?"

"She is," answered Tord, quite untroubled. "In stormy weather she rides out on a sea to meet the ships over which the waves are washing, and those who are carried overboard are hers."

"What does she do with them?" asked Berg.

"Oh, a witch always needs corpses. She makes ointments out of them, or perhaps she eats them. On moonlight nights she sits in the surf, where it is whitest, and the spray dashes over her. They say that she sits and searches for shipwrecked children's fingers and eyes."

"That is awful," said Berg.

The boy answered with infinite assurance: "That would be awful in others, but not in witches. They have to do so."

Berg Rese found that he had here come upon a new way of regarding the world and things.

"Do thieves have to steal, as witches have to use witchcraft?" he asked sharply.

"Yes, of course," answered the boy; "everyone has to do what he is destined to do." But then he added, with a cautious smile: "There are thieves also who have never stolen."

"Say out what you mean," said Berg.

The boy continued with his mysterious smile, proud at being an unsolvable riddle: "It is like speaking of birds who do not fly to talk of thieves who do not steal."

Berg Rese pretended to be stupid in order to find out what he wanted. "No one can be called a thief without having stolen," he said.

"No; but," said the boy, and pressed his lips together as if to keep in the words, "but if someone had a father who stole," he hinted after a while.

"One inherits money and lands," replied Berg Rese, "but no one bears the name of thief if he has not himself earned it."

Tord laughed quietly. "But if somebody has a mother who begs and prays him to take his father's crime on him. But if such a one cheats the hangman and escapes to the woods. But if someone is made an outlaw for a fish-net which he has never seen."

Berg Rese struck the stone table with his clenched fist. He was angry. This fair young man had thrown away his whole life. He could never win love, nor riches, nor esteem after that. The wretched striving for food and clothes was all which was left him. And the fool had let him, Berg Rese, go on despising one who was innocent. He rebuked him with stern words, but Tord was not even as afraid as a sick child is of its mother, when she chides it because it has caught cold by wading in the spring brooks.

* * * * *

On one of the broad, wooded mountains lay a dark tarn. It was square, with as straight shores and as sharp corners as if it had been cut by the hand of man. On three sides it was surrounded by steep cliffs, on which pines clung with roots as thick as a man's arm. Down by the pool, where the earth had been gradually washed away, their roots stood up out of the water, bare and crooked and wonderfully twisted about one another. It was like an infinite number of serpents which had wanted all at the same time to crawl up out of the pool but had got entangled in one another and been held fast. Or it was like a mass of blackened skeletons of drowned giants which the pool wanted to throw up on the land. Arms and legs writhed about one another, the long fingers dug deep into the very cliff to get a hold, the mighty ribs formed arches, which held up primeval trees. It had happened, however, that the iron arms, the steel-like fingers with which the pines held themselves fast, had given way, and a pine had been borne by a mighty north wind from the top of the cliff down into the pool. It had burrowed deep down into the muddy bottom with its top and now stood there. The smaller fish had a good place of refuge among its branches, but the roots stuck up above the water like a many-armed monster and contributed to make the pool awful and terrifying.

On the tarn's fourth side the cliff sank down. There a little foaming stream carried away its waters. Before this stream could find the only possible way, it had tried to get out between stones and tufts, and had by so doing made a little world of islands, some no bigger than a little hillock, others covered with trees.

Here where the encircling cliffs did not shut out all the sun, leafy trees flourished. Here stood thirsty, gray-green alders and smooth-leaved willows. The birch-tree grew there as it does everywhere where it is trying to crowd out the pine woods, and the wild cherry and the mountain ash, those two which edge the forest pastures, filling them with fragrance and adorning them with beauty.

Here at the outlet there was a forest of reeds as high as a man, which made the sunlight fall green on the water just as it falls on the moss in the real forest. Among the reeds there were open places; small, round pools, and water-lilies were floating there. The tall stalks looked down with mild seriousness on those sensitive beauties, who discontentedly shut their white petals and yellow stamens in a hard, leather-like sheath as soon as the sun ceased to show itself.

One sunshiny day the outlaws came to this tarn to fish. They waded out to a couple of big stones in the midst of the reed forest and sat there and threw out bait for the big, green-striped pickerel that lay and slept near the surface of the water.

These men, who were always wandering in the woods and the mountains, had, without their knowing it themselves, come under nature's rule as much as the plants and the animals. When the sun shone, they were open-hearted and brave, but in the evening, as soon as the sun had disappeared, they became silent; and the night, which seemed to them much greater and more powerful than the day, made them anxious and helpless. Now the green light, which slanted in between the rushes and coloured the water with brown and dark-green streaked with gold, affected their mood until they were ready for any miracle. Every outlook was shut off. Sometimes the reeds rocked in an imperceptible wind, their stalks rustled, and the long, ribbon-like leaves fluttered against their faces. They sat in grey skins on the grey stones. The shadows in the skins repeated the shadows of the weather-beaten, mossy stone. Each saw his companion in his silence and immovability change into a stone image. But in among the rushes swam mighty fishes with rainbow-coloured backs. When the men threw out their hooks and saw the circles spreading among the reeds, it seemed as if the motion grew stronger and stronger, until they perceived that it was not caused only by their cast. A sea-nymph, half human, half a shining fish, lay and slept on the surface of the water. She lay on her back with her whole body under water. The waves so nearly covered her that they had not noticed her before. It was her breathing that caused the motion of the waves. But there was nothing strange in her lying there, and when the next instant she was gone, they were not sure that she had not been only an illusion.

The green light entered through the eyes into the brain like a gentle intoxication. The men sat and stared with dulled thoughts, seeing visions among the reeds, of which they did not dare to tell one another. Their catch was poor. The day was devoted to dreams and apparitions.

The stroke of oars was heard among the rushes, and they started up as from sleep. The next moment a flat-bottomed boat appeared, heavy, hollowed out with no skill and with oars as small as sticks. A young girl, who had been picking water-lilies, rowed it. She had dark-brown hair, gathered in great braids, and big dark eyes; otherwise she was strangely pale. But her paleness toned to pink and not to grey. Her cheeks had no higher colour than the rest of her face, the lips had hardly enough. She wore a white linen shirt and a leather belt with a gold buckle. Her skirt was blue with a red hem. She rowed by the outlaws without seeing them. They kept breathlessly still, but not for fear of being seen, but only to be able to really see her. As soon as she had gone they were as if changed from stone images to living beings. Smiling, they looked at one another.

"She was white like the water-lilies," said one. "Her eyes were as dark as the water there under the pine-roots."

They were so excited that they wanted to laugh, really laugh as no one had ever laughed by that pool, till the cliffs thundered with echoes and the roots of the pines loosened with fright.

"Did you think she was pretty?" asked Berg Rese.

"Oh, I do not know, I saw her for such a short time. Perhaps she was."

"I do not believe you dared to look at her. You thought that it was a mermaid."

And they were again shaken by the same extravagant merriment.

* * * * *

Tord had once as a child seen a drowned man. He had found the body on the shore on a summer day and had not been at all afraid, but at night he had dreamed terrible dreams. He saw a sea, where every wave rolled a dead man to his feet. He saw, too, that all the islands were covered with drowned men, who were dead and belonged to the sea, but who still could speak and move and threaten him with withered white hands.

It was so with him now. The girl whom he had seen among the rushes came back in his dreams. He met her out in the open pool, where the sunlight fell even greener than among the rushes, and he had time to see that she was beautiful. He dreamed that he had crept up on the big pine root in the middle of the dark tarn, but the pine swayed and rocked so that sometimes he was quite under water. Then she came forward on the little islands. She stood under the red mountain ashes and laughed at him. In the last dream-vision he had come so far that she kissed him. It was already morning, and he heard that Berg Rese had got up, but he obstinately shut his eyes to be able to go on with his dream. When he awoke, he was as though dizzy and stunned by what had happened to him in the night. He thought much more now of the girl than he had done the day before.

Toward night he happened to ask Berg Rese if he knew her name.

Berg looked at him inquiringly. "Perhaps it is best for you to hear it," he said. "She is Unn. We are cousins."

Tord then knew that it was for that pale girl's sake Berg Rese wandered an outlaw in forest and mountain. Tord tried to remember what he knew of her. Unn was the daughter of a rich peasant. Her mother was dead, so that she managed her father's house. This she liked, for she was fond of her own way and she had no wish to be married.

Unn and Berg Rese were the children of brothers, and it had been long said that Berg preferred to sit with Unn and her maids and jest with them than to work on his own lands. When the great Christmas feast was celebrated at his house, his wife had invited a monk from Draksmark, for she wanted him to remonstrate with Berg, because he was forgetting her for another woman. This monk was hateful to Berg and to many on account of his appearance. He was very fat and quite white. The ring of hair about his bald head, the eyebrows above his watery eyes, his face, his hands and his whole cloak, everything was white. Many found it hard to endure his looks.

At the banquet table, in the hearing of all the guests, this monk now said, for he was fearless and thought that his words would have more effect if they were heard by many, "People are in the habit of saying that the cuckoo is the worst of birds because he does not rear his young in his own nest, but here sits a man who does not provide for his home and his children, but seeks his pleasure with a strange woman. Him will I call the worst of men." Unn then rose up. "That, Berg, is said to you and me," she said. "Never have I been so insulted, and my father is not here either." She had wished to go, but Berg sprang after her. "Do not move!" she said. "I will never see you again." He caught up with her in the hall and asked her what he should do to make her stay. She had answered with flashing eyes that he must know that best himself. Then Berg went in and killed the monk.

Berg and Tord were busy with the same thoughts, for after a while Berg said: "You should have seen her, Unn, when the white monk fell. The mistress of the house gathered the small children about her and cursed her. She turned their faces toward her, that they might forever remember her who had made their father a murderer. But Unn stood calm and so beautiful that the men trembled. She thanked me for the deed and told me to fly to the woods. She bade me not to be robber, and not to use the knife until I could do it for an equally just cause."

"Your deed had been to her honour," said Tord.

Berg Rese noticed again what had astonished him before in the boy. He was like a heathen, worse than a heathen; he never condemned what was wrong. He felt no responsibility. That which must be, was. He knew of God and Christ and the saints, but only by name, as one knows the gods of foreign lands. The ghosts of the rocks were his gods. His mother, wise in witchcraft, had taught him to believe in the spirits of the dead.

Then Berg Rese undertook a task which was as foolish as to twist a rope about his own neck. He set before those ignorant eyes the great God, the Lord of justice, the Avenger of misdeeds, who casts the wicked into places of everlasting torment. And he taught him to love Christ and his mother and the holy men and women, who with lifted hands kneeled before God's throne to avert the wrath of the great Avenger from the hosts of sinners. He taught him all that men do to appease God's wrath. He showed him the crowds of pilgrims making pilgrimages to holy places, the flight of self-torturing penitents and monks from a worldly life.

As he spoke, the boy became more eager and more pale, his eyes grew large as if for terrible visions. Berg Rese wished to stop, but thoughts streamed to him, and he went on speaking. The night sank down over them, the black forest night, when the owls hoot. God came so near to them that they saw his throne darken the stars, and the chastising angels sank down to the tops of the trees. And under them the fires of Hell flamed up to the earth's crust, eagerly licking that shaking place of refuge for the sorrowing races of men.

* * * * *

The autumn had come with a heavy storm. Tord went alone in the woods to see after the snares and traps. Berg Rese sat at home to mend his clothes. Tord's way led in a broad path up a wooded height.

Every gust carried the dry leaves in a rustling whirl up the path. Time after time Tord thought that someone went behind him. He often looked round. Sometimes he stopped to listen, but he understood that it was the leaves and the wind, and went on. As soon as he started on again, he heard someone come dancing on silken foot up the slope. Small feet came tripping. Elves and fairies played behind him. When he turned round, there was no one, always no one. He shook his fists at the rustling leaves and went on.

They did not grow silent for that, but they took another tone. Then began to hiss and to pant behind him. A big viper came gliding. Its tongue dripping venom hung far out of its mouth, and its bright body shone against the withered leaves. Beside the snake pattered a wolf, a big, gaunt monster, who was ready to seize fast in his throat when the snake had twisted about his feet and bitten Him in the heel. Sometimes they were both silent, as if to approach him unperceived, but they soon betrayed themselves by hissing and panting, and sometimes the wolf's claws rang against a stone. Involuntarily

Tord walked quicker and quicker, but the creatures hastened after him. When he felt that they were only two steps distant and were preparing to strike, he turned. There was nothing there, and he had known it the whole time.

He sat down on a stone to rest. Then the dry leaves played about his feet as if to amuse him. All the leaves of the forest were there: small, light yellow birch leaves, red speckled mountain ash, the elm's dry, dark-brown leaves, the aspen's tough light red, and the willow's yellow green. Transformed and withered, scarred and torn were they, and much unlike the downy, light green, delicately shaped leaves which a few months ago had rolled out of their buds.

"Sinners," said the boy, "sinners, nothing is pure in God's eyes. The flame of his wrath has already reached you."

When he resumed his wandering, he saw the forest under him bend before the storm like a heaving sea, but in the path it was calm. But he heard what he did not feel. The woods were full of voices.

He heard whisperings, wailing songs, coarse threats, thundering oaths. There were laughter and laments, there was the noise of many people. That which hounded and pursued, which rustled and hissed, which seemed to be something and still was nothing, gave him wild thoughts. He felt again the anguish of death, as when he lay on the floor in his den and the peasants hunted him through the wood. He heard again the crashing of branches, the people's heavy tread, the ring of weapons, the resounding cries, the wild, bloodthirsty noise, which followed the crowd.

But it was not only that which he heard in the storm. There was something else, something still more terrible, voices which he could not interpret, a confusion of voices, which seemed to him to speak in foreign tongues. He had heard mightier storms than this whistle through the rigging, but never before had he heard the wind play on such a many-voiced harp. Each tree had its own voice; the pine did not murmur like the aspen nor the poplar like the mountain ash. Every hole had its note, every cliff's sounding echo its own ring. And the noise of the brooks and the cry of foxes mingled with the marvellous forest storm. But all that he could interpret; there were other strange sounds. It was those which made him begin to scream and scoff and groan in emulation with the storm.

He had always been afraid when he was alone in the darkness of the forest. He liked the open sea and the bare rocks. Spirits and phantoms crept about among the trees.

Suddenly he heard who it was who spoke in the storm. It was God, the great Avenger, the God of justice. He was hunting him for the sake of his comrade. He demanded that he should deliver up the murderer to His vengeance.

Then Tord began to speak in the midst of the storm. He told God what he had wished to do, but had not been able. He had wished to speak to Berg Rese and to beg him to make his peace with God, but he had been too shy. Bashfulness had made him dumb. "When I heard that the earth was ruled by a just God," he cried, "I understood that he was a lost man. I have lain and wept for my friend many long nights. I knew that God would find him out, wherever he might hide. But I could not speak, nor teach him to understand. I was speechless, because I loved him so much. Ask not that I shall speak to him, ask not that the sea shall rise up against the mountain."

He was silent, and in the storm the deep voice, which had been the voice of God for him, ceased. It was suddenly calm, with a sharp sun and a splashing as of oars and a gentle rustle as of stiff rushes. These sounds brought Unn's image before him. The outlaw cannot have anything, not riches, nor women, nor the esteem of men. If he should betray Berg, he would be taken under the protection of the law. But Unn must love Berg, after what he had done for her. There was no way out of it all.

When the storm increased, he heard again steps behind him and sometimes a breathless panting. Now he did not dare to look back, for he knew that the white monk went behind him. He came from the feast at Berg Rese's house, drenched with blood, with a gaping axe-wound in his forehead. And he whispered: "Denounce him, betray him, save his soul. Leave his body to the pyre, that his soul may be spared. Leave him to the slow torture of the rack, that his soul may have time to repent."

Tord ran. All this fright of what was nothing in itself grew, when it so continually played on the soul, to an unspeakable terror. He wished to escape from it all. As he began to run, again thundered that deep, terrible voice which was God's. God himself hunted him with alarms, that he should give up the murderer. Berg Rese's crime seemed more detestable than ever to him. An unarmed man had been murdered, a man of God pierced with shining steel. It was like a defiance of the Lord of the world. And the murderer dared to live! He rejoiced in the sun's light and in the fruits of the earth as if the Almighty's arm were too short to reach him.

He stopped, clenched his fists and howled out a threat. Then he ran like a madman from the wood down to the valley.

* * * * *

Tord hardly needed to tell his errand; instantly ten peasants were ready to follow him. It was decided that Tord should go alone up to the cave, so that Berg's suspicions should not be aroused. But where he went he should scatter peas, so that the peasants could find the way.

When Tord came to the cave, the outlaw sat on the stone bench and sewed. The fire gave hardly any light, and the work seemed to go badly. The boy's heart swelled with pity. The splendid Berg Rese seemed to him poor and unhappy. And the only thing he possessed, his life, should be taken from him. Tord began to weep.

"What is it?" asked Berg. "Are you ill? Have you been frightened?"

Then for the first time Tord spoke of his fear. "It was terrible in the wood. I heard ghosts and saw spectres. I saw white monks."

"'Sdeath, boy!"

"They crowded round me all the way up Broad mountain. I ran, but they followed after and sang. Can I never be rid of the sound? What have I to do with them? I think that they could go to one who needed it more."

"Are you mad to-night, Tord?"

Tord talked, hardly knowing what words he used. He was free from all shyness. The words streamed from his lips.

"They are all white monks, white, pale as death. They all have blood on their cloaks. They drag their hoods down over their brows, but still the wound shines from under; the big, red, gaping wound from the blow of the axe."

"The big, red, gaping wound from the blow of the axe?"

"Is it I who perhaps have struck it? Why shall I see it?"

"The saints only know, Tord," said Berg Rese, pale and with terrible earnestness, "what it means that you see a wound from an axe. I killed the monk with a couple of knife-thrusts."

Tord stood trembling before Berg and wrung his hands. "They demand you of me! They want to force me to betray you!"

"Who? The monks?"

"They, yes, the monks. They show me visions. They show me her, Unn. They show me the shining, sunny sea. They show me the fisherman's camping-ground, where there is dancing and merry-making. I close my eyes, but still I see. 'Leave me in peace,' I say. 'My friend has murdered, but he is not bad. Let me be, and I will talk to him, so that he repents and atones. He shall confess his sin and go to Christ's grave. We will both go together to the places which are so holy that all sin is taken away from him who draws near them.'"

"What do the monks answer?" asked Berg. "They want to have me saved. They want to have me on the rack and wheel."

"Shall I betray my dearest friend, I ask them," continued Tord. "He is my world. He has saved me from the bear that had his paw on my throat. We have been cold together and suffered every want together. He has spread his bearskin over me when I was sick. I have carried wood and water for him; I have watched over him while he slept; I have fooled his enemies. Why do they think that I am one who will betray a friend? My friend will soon of his own accord go to the priest and confess, then we will go together to the land of atonement."

Berg listened earnestly, his eyes sharply searching Tord's face. "You shall go to the priest and tell him the truth," he said. "You need to be among people."

"Does that help me if I go alone? For your sin, Death and all his spectres follow me. Do you not see how I shudder at you? You have lifted your hand against God himself. No crime is like yours. I think that I must rejoice when I see you on rack and wheel. It is well for him who can receive his punishment in this world and escapes the wrath to come. Why did you tell me of the just God? You compel me to betray you. Save me from that sin. Go to the priest." And he fell on his knees before Berg.

The murderer laid his hand on his head and looked at him. He was measuring his sin against his friend's anguish, and it grew big and terrible before his soul. He saw himself at variance with the Will which rules the world. Repentance entered his heart.

"Woe to me that I have done what I have done," he said. "That which awaits me is too hard to meet voluntarily. If I give myself up to the priests, they will torture me for hours; they will roast me with slow fires. And is not this life of misery, which we lead in fear and want, penance enough? Have I not lost lands and home? Do I not live parted from friends and everything which makes a man's happiness? What more is required?"

When he spoke so, Tord sprang up wild with terror. "Can you repent?" he cried. "Can my words move your heart? Then come instantly! How could I believe that! Let us escape! There is still time."

Berg Rese sprang up, he too. "You have done it, then——"

"Yes, yes, yes! I have betrayed you! But come quickly! Come, as you can repent! They will let us go. We shall escape them!"

The murderer bent down to the floor, where the battle-axe of his ancestors lay at his feet. "You son of a thief!" he said, hissing out the words, "I have trusted you and loved you."

But when Tord saw him bend for the axe, he knew that it was now a question of his own life. He snatched his own axe from his belt and struck at Berg before he had time to raise himself. The edge cut through the whistling air and sank in the bent head. Berg Rese fell head foremost to the floor, his body rolled after. Blood and brains spouted out, the axe fell from the wound. In the matted hair Tord saw a big, red, gaping hole from the blow of an axe.

The peasants came rushing in. They rejoiced and praised the deed.

"You will win by this," they said to Tord.

Tord looked down at his hands as if he saw there the fetters with which he had been dragged forward to kill him he loved. They were forged from nothing. Of the rushes' green light, of the play of the shadows, of the song of the storm, of the rustling of the leaves, of dreams were they created. And he said aloud: "God is great."

But again the old thought came to him. He fell on his knees beside the body and put his arm under his head.

"Do him no harm," he said. "He repents; he is going to the Holy Sepulchre. He is not dead, he is not a prisoner. We were just ready to go when he fell. The white monk did not want him to repent, but God, the God of justice, loves repentance."

He lay beside the body, talked to it, wept and begged the dead man to awake. The peasants arranged a bier. They wished to carry the peasant's body down to his house. They had respect for the dead and spoke softly in his presence. When they lifted him up on the bier, Tord rose, shook the hair back from his face, and said with a voice which shook with sobs,—

"Say to Unn, who made Berg Rese a murderer, that he was killed by Tord the fisherman, whose father is a wrecker and whose mother is a witch, because he taught him that the foundation of the world is justice."

IV

THE PRINCESS BOB AND HER FRIENDS*

BRET HARTE

*Reprinted by permission of, and by special arrangement with Houghton Mifflin Co.

She was a Klamath Indian. Her title was, I think, a compromise between her claim as daughter of a chief and gratitude to her earliest white protector, whose name, after the Indian fashion, she had adopted. "Bob" Walker had taken her from the breast of her dead mother at a time when the sincere volunteer soldiery of the California frontier were impressed with the belief that extermination was the manifest destiny of the Indian race. He had with difficulty restrained the noble zeal of his compatriots long enough to convince them that the exemption of one Indian baby would not invalidate this theory. And he took her to his home,—a pastoral clearing on the banks of the Salmon River,—where she was cared for after a frontier fashion.

Before she was nine years old, she had exhausted the scant kindliness of the thin, overworked Mrs. Walker. As a playfellow of the young Walkers she was unreliable; as a nurse for the baby she was inefficient. She lost the former in the trackless depths of a redwood forest; she basely abandoned the latter in an extemporized cradle, hanging like a chrysalis to a convenient bough. She lied and she stole,—two unpardonable sins in a frontier community, where truth was a necessity and provisions were the only property. Worse than this, the outskirts of the clearing were sometimes haunted by blanketed tatterdemalions with whom she had mysterious confidences. Mr. Walker more than once regretted his indiscreet humanity; but she presently relieved him of responsibility, and possibly of blood-guiltiness, by disappearing entirely.

When she reappeared, it was at the adjacent village of Logport, in the capacity of housemaid to a trader's wife, who, joining some little culture to considerable conscientiousness, attempted to instruct her charge. But the Princess proved an unsatisfactory pupil to even so liberal a teacher. She accepted the alphabet with great good-humour, but always as a pleasing and recurring novelty, in which all interest expired at the completion of each lesson. She found a thousand uses for her books and writing materials other than those known to civilized children. She made a curious necklace of bits of slate-pencil, she constructed a miniature canoe from the pasteboard covers of her primer, she bent her pens into fish-hooks, and tattooed the faces of her younger companions with blue ink. Religious instruction she received as good-humouredly, and learned to pronounce the name of the Deity with a cheerful familiarity that shocked her preceptress. Nor could her reverence be reached through analogy; she knew nothing of the Great Spirit, and professed entire ignorance of the Happy Hunting-Grounds. Yet she attended divine service regularly, and as regularly asked for a hymn-book; and it was only through the discovery that she had collected twenty-five of these volumes and had hidden them behind the woodpile, that her connection with the First Baptist Church of Logport ceased. She would occasionally abandon these civilized and Christian privileges, and disappear from her home, returning after several days of absence with an odour of bark and fish, and a peace-offering to her mistress in the shape of venison or game.

To add to her troubles, she was now fourteen, and, according to the laws of her race, a woman. I do not think the most romantic fancy would have called her pretty. Her complexion defied most of those ambiguous similes through which poets unconsciously apologize for any deviation from the Caucasian standard. It was not wine nor amber coloured; if anything, it was smoky. Her face was tatooed with red and white lines on one cheek, as if a fine-toothed comb had been drawn from cheek-bone to jaw, and, but for the good-humour that beamed from her small berry-like eyes and shone in her white teeth, would have been repulsive. She was short and stout. In her scant drapery and unrestrained freedom she was hardly statuesque, and her more unstudied attitudes were marred by a simian habit of softly scratching her left ankle with the toes of her right foot, in moments of contemplation.

I think I have already shown enough to indicate the incongruity of her existence with even the low standard of civilization that obtained at Logport in the year 1860. It needed but one more fact to prove the far-sighted political sagacity and prophetic ethics of those sincere advocates of extermination to whose virtues I have done but scant justice in the beginning of this article. This fact was presently furnished by the Princess. After one of her periodical disappearances—this time unusually prolonged—she astonished Logport by returning with a half-breed baby of a week old in her arms. That night a meeting of the hard-featured serious matrons of Logport was held at Mrs. Brown's. The immediate banishment of the Princess was demanded. Soft-hearted Mrs. Brown endeavoured vainly to get a mitigation or suspension of the sentence. But, as on a former occasion, the Princess took matters into her own hands. A few mornings afterwards a wicker cradle containing an Indian baby was found hanging on the handle of the door of the First Baptist Church. It was the Parthian arrow of the flying Princess. From that day Logport knew her no more.

It had been a bright clear day on the upland, so clear that the ramparts of Fort Jackson and the flagstaff were plainly visible twelve miles away from the long curving peninsula that stretched a bared white arm around the peaceful waters of Logport Bay. It had been a clear day upon the seashore, albeit the air was filled with the flying spume and shifting sand of a straggling beach whose low dunes were dragged down by the long surges of the Pacific and thrown up again by the tumultuous tradewinds. But the sun had gone down in a bank of fleecy fog that was beginning to roll in upon the beach. Gradually the headland at the entrance of the harbour and the lighthouse disappeared, then the willow fringe that marked the line of Salmon River vanished, and the ocean was gone. A few sails still gleamed on the waters of the bay; but the advancing fog wiped them out one by one, crept across the steel-blue expanse, swallowed up the white mills and single spire of Logport, and, joining with reinforcements from the marshes, moved solemnly upon the hills. Ten minutes more and the landscape was utterly blotted out; simultaneously the wind died away, and a death-like silence stole over sea and shore. The faint clang, high overhead, of unseen brent, the nearer call of invisible plover, the lap and wash of undistinguishable waters, and the monotonous roll of the vanished ocean, were the only sounds. As night deepened, the far-off booming of the fog-bell on the headland at intervals stirred the thick air.

Hard by the shore of the bay, and half hidden by a drifting sand-hill, stood a low nondescript structure, to whose composition sea and shore had equally contributed. It was built partly of logs and partly of driftwood and tarred canvas. Joined to one end of the main building—the ordinary log-cabin of the settler—was the half-round pilot-house of some wrecked steamer, while the other gable terminated in half of a broken whaleboat. Nailed against the boat were the dried skins of wild animals, and scattered about lay the flotsam and jetsam of many years' gathering,—bamboo crates, casks, hatches, blocks, oars, boxes, part of a whale's vertebræ, and the blades of swordfish. Drawn up on the beach of a little cove before the house lay a canoe. As the night thickened and the fog grew more dense, these details grew imperceptible, and only the windows of the pilot-house, lit up by a roaring fire within the hut, gleamed redly through the mist.

By this fire, beneath a ship's lamp that swung from the roof, two figures were seated, a man and a woman. The man, broad-shouldered and heavily bearded, stretched his listless powerful length beyond a broken bamboo chair, with his eyes fixed on the fire. The woman couched cross-legged upon the broad earthen hearth, with her eyes blinkingly fixed on her companion. They were small, black, round, berry-like eyes, and as the firelight shone upon her smoky face, with its one striped cheek of gorgeous brilliancy, it was plainly the Princess Bob and no other.

Not a word was spoken. They had been sitting thus for more than an hour, and there was about their attitude a suggestion that silence was habitual. Once or twice the man rose and walked up and down the narrow room, or gazed absently from the windows of the pilot-house, but never by look or sign betrayed the slightest consciousness of his companion. At such times the Princess from her nest by the fire followed him with eyes of canine expectancy and wistfulness. But he would as inevitably return to his contemplation of the fire, and the Princess to her blinking watchfulness of his face.

They had sat there silent and undisturbed for many an evening in fair weather and foul. They had spent many a day in the sunshine and storm, gathering the unclaimed spoil of sea and shore. They had kept these mute relations, varied only by the incidents of the hunt or meagre household duties, for three years, ever since the man, wandering moodily over the lonely sands, had fallen upon the half-starved woman lying in the little hollow where she had crawled to die. It had seemed as if they would never be disturbed, until now, when the Princess started, and, with the instinct of her race, bent her ear to the ground.

The wind had risen and was rattling the tarred canvas. But in another moment there plainly came from without the hut the sound of voices. Then followed a rap at the door; then another rap; and then, before they could rise to their feet, the door was flung briskly open.

"I beg your pardon," said a pleasant but somewhat decided contralto voice, "but I don't think you heard me knock. Ah, I see you did not. May I come in?"

There was no reply. Had the battered figurehead of the Goddess of Liberty, which lay deeply embedded in the sand on the beach, suddenly appeared at the door demanding admittance, the occupants of the cabin could not have been more speechlessly and hopelessly astonished than at the form which stood in the open doorway.

It was that of a slim, shapely, elegantly dressed young woman. A scarlet-lined silken hood was half thrown back from the shining mass of the black hair that covered her small head; from her pretty shoulders drooped a fur cloak, only restrained by a cord and tassel in her small gloved hand. Around her full throat was a double necklace of large white beads, that by some cunning feminine trick relieved with its infantile suggestion the strong decision of her lower face.

"Did you say yes? Ah, thank you. We may come in, Barker." (Here a shadow in a blue army overcoat followed her into the cabin, touched its cap respectfully, and then stood silent and erect against the wall.) "Don't disturb yourself in the least, I beg. What a distressingly unpleasant night! Is this your usual climate?"

Half graciously, half absently overlooking the still embarrassed silence of the group, she went on: "We started from the fort over three hours ago,—three hours ago, wasn't it, Barker?" (the erect Barker touched his cap)—"to go to Captain Emmons's quarters on Indian Island,—I think you call it Indian Island, don't you?" (she was appealing to the awe-stricken Princess),—"and we got into the fog and lost our way; that is, Barker lost his way" (Barker touched his cap deprecatingly), "and goodness knows where we didn't wander to until we mistook your light for the lighthouse and pulled up here. No, no, pray keep your seat, do! Really I must insist."

Nothing could exceed the languid grace of the latter part of this speech,—nothing except the easy unconsciousness with which she glided by the offered chair of her stammering, embarrassed host and stood beside the open hearth.

"Barker will tell you," she continued, warming her feet by the fire, "that I am Miss Portfire, daughter of Major Portfire, commanding the post. Ah, excuse me, child!" (She had accidentally trodden upon the bare yellow toes of the Princess.) "Really, I did not know you were there. I am very near-sighted." (In confirmation of her statement, she put to her eyes a dainty double eyeglass that dangled from her neck.) "It's a shocking thing to be near-sighted, isn't it?"

If the shamefaced uneasy man to whom this remark was addressed could have found words to utter the thought that even in his confusion struggled uppermost in his mind, he would, looking at the bold, dark eyes that questioned, have denied the fact. But he only stammered, "Yes." The next moment, however, Miss Portfire had apparently forgotten him and was examining the Princess through her glass.

"And what is your name, child?"

The Princess, beatified by the eyes and eyeglass, showed all her white teeth at once, and softly scratched her leg.

"Bob."

"Bob? What a singular name!"

Miss Portfire's host here hastened to explain the origin of the Princess's title.

"Then you are Bob." (Eyeglass.)

"No, my name is Grey,—John Grey." And he actually achieved a bow where awkwardness was rather the air of imperfectly recalling a forgotten habit.

"Grey?—ah, let me see. Yes, certainly. You are Mr. Grey the recluse, the hermit, the philosopher, and all that sort of thing. Why, certainly; Dr. Jones, our surgeon, has told me all about you. Dear me, how interesting a rencontre! Lived all alone here for seven—was it seven years?—yes, I remember now. Existed quite *au naturel*, one might say. How odd! Not that I know anything about that sort of thing, you know. I've lived always among people, and am really quite a stranger, I assure you. But honestly, Mr.—I beg your pardon—Mr. Grey, how do you like it?"

She had quietly taken his chair and thrown her cloak and hood over its back, and was now thoughtfully removing her gloves. Whatever were the arguments,—and they were doubtless many and profound,—whatever the experience,—and it was doubtless hard and satisfying enough,—by which this unfortunate man had justified his life for the last seven years, somehow they suddenly became trivial and terribly ridiculous before this simple but practical question.

"Well, you shall tell me all about it after you have given me something to eat. We will have time enough; Barker cannot find his way back in this fog to-night. Now don't put yourselves to any trouble on my account. Barker will assist."

Barker came forward. Glad to escape the scrutiny of his guest, the hermit gave a few rapid directions to the Princess in her native tongue, and disappeared in the shed. Left a moment alone, Miss Portfire took a quick, half-audible, feminine inventory of the cabin. "Books, guns, skins, *one* chair, *one* bed, no pictures, and no looking-glass!" She took a book from the swinging shelf and resumed her seat by the fire as the Princess re-entered with fresh fuel. But while kneeling on the hearth the Princess chanced to look up and met Miss Portfire's dark eyes over the edge of her book.

"Bob!"

The Princess showed her teeth.

"Listen. Would you like to have fine clothes, rings, and beads like these, to have your hair nicely combed and put up so? Would you?"

The Princess nodded violently.

"Would you like to live with me and have them? Answer quickly. Don't look round for him. Speak for yourself. Would you? Hush; never mind now."

The hermit re-entered, and the Princess, blinking, retreated into the shadow of the whaleboat shed, from which she did not emerge even when the homely repast of cold venison, ship biscuit, and tea was served. Miss Portfire noticed her absence: "You really must not let me interfere with your usual simple ways. Do you know this is exceedingly interesting to me, so pastoral and patriarchal and all that sort of thing. I must insist upon the Princess coming back; really, I must."

But the Princess was not to be found in the shed, and Miss Portfire, who the next minute seemed to have forgotten all about her, took her place in the single chair before an extemporized table. Barker stood behind her, and the hermit leaned against the fireplace. Miss Portfire's appetite did not come up to her protestations. For the first time in seven years it occurred to the hermit that his ordinary victual might be improved. He stammered out something to that effect.

"I have eaten better, and worse," said Miss Portfire, quietly.

"But I thought you—that is, you said——"

"I spent a year in the hospitals, when father was on the Potomac," returned Miss Portfire, composedly. After a pause she continued: "You remember after the second Bull Run— But, dear me! I beg your pardon; of course, you know nothing about the war and all that sort of thing, and don't care." (She put up her eyeglass and quietly surveyed his broad muscular figure against the chimney.) "Or, perhaps, your prejudices— But then, as a hermit you know you have no politics, of course. Please don't let me bore you."

To have been strictly consistent, the hermit should have exhibited no interest in this topic. Perhaps it was owing to some quality in the narrator, but he was constrained to beg her to continue in such phrases as his unfamiliar lips could command. So that little by little Miss Portfire yielded up incident and personal observation of contest then raging; with the same half-abstracted, half-unconcerned air that seemed habitual to her, she told the stories of privation, of suffering, of endurance, and of sacrifice. With the same assumption of timid deference that concealed her great self-control, she talked of principles and rights. Apparently without enthusiasm and without effort, of which his morbid nature would have been suspicious, she sang the great American Iliad in a way that stirred the depths of her solitary auditor to its massive foundations. Then she stopped and asked quietly, "Where is Bob?"

The hermit started. He would look for her. But Bob, for some reason, was not forthcoming. Search was made within and without the hut, but in vain. For the first time that evening Miss Portfire showed some anxiety. "Go," she said to Barker, "and find her. She *must* be found; stay, give me your overcoat, I'll go myself." She threw the overcoat over her shoulders and stepped out into the night. In the thick veil of fog that seemed suddenly to inwrap her, she stood for a moment irresolute, and then walked toward the beach, guided by the low wash of waters on the sand. She had not taken many steps before she stumbled over some dark crouching object. Reaching down her hand she felt the coarse wiry mane of the Princess.

"Bob!"

There was no reply.

"Bob. I've been looking for you, come."

"Go 'way."

"Nonsense, Bob. I want you to stay with me to-night, come."

"Injin squaw no good for waugee woman. Go 'way."

"Listen, Bob. You are daughter of a chief: so am I. Your father had many warriors: so has mine. It is good that you stay with me. Come."

The Princess chuckled and suffered herself to be lifted up. A few moments later they re-entered the hut hand in hand.

With the first red streaks of dawn the next day the erect Barker touched his cap at the door of the hut. Beside him stood the hermit, also just risen from his blanketed nest in the sand. Forth from the hut, fresh as the morning air, stepped Miss Portfire, leading the Princess by the hand. Hand in hand also they walked to the shore, and when the Princess had been safely bestowed in the stern sheets, Miss Portfire turned and held out her own to her late host.

"I shall take the best of care of her, of course. You will come and see her often. I should ask you to come and see me, but you are a hermit, you know, and all that sort of thing. But if it's the correct anchorite thing, and can be done, my father will be glad to requite you for this night's hospitality. But don't do anything on my account that interferes with your simple habits. Good-bye."

She handed him a card, which he took mechanically.

"Good-bye."

The sail was hoisted, and the boat shoved off. As the fresh morning breeze caught the white canvas it seemed to bow a parting salutation. There was a rosy flush of promise on the water, and as the light craft darted forward toward the ascending sun, it seemed for a moment uplifted in its glory.

Miss Portfire kept her word. If thoughtful care and intelligent kindness could regenerate the Princess, her future was secure. And it really seemed as if she were for the first time inclined to heed the lessons of civilization and profit by her new condition. An agreeable change was first noticed in her appearance. Her lawless hair was caught in a net, and no longer strayed over her low forehead. Her unstable bust was stayed and upheld by French corsets; her plantigrade shuffle was limited by heeled boots. Her dresses were neat and clean, and she wore a double necklace of glass beads. With this physical improvement there also seemed some moral awakening. She no longer stole nor lied. With the possession of personal property came a respect for that of others. With increased dependence on the word of those about her came a thoughtful consideration of her own. Intellectually she was still feeble, although she grappled sturdily with the simple lessons which Miss Portfire set before her. But her zeal and simple vanity outran her discretion, and she would often sit for hours with an open book before her, which she could not read. She was a favourite with the officers at the fort, from the Major, who shared his daughter's prejudices and often yielded to her powerful self-will, to the subalterns, who liked her none the less that their natural enemies, the frontier volunteers, had declared war against her helpless sisterhood. The only restraint put upon her was the limitation of her liberty to the enclosure of the fort and parade; and only once did she break this parole, and was stopped by the sentry as she stepped into a boat at the landing.

The recluse did not avail himself of Miss Portfire's invitation. But after the departure of the Princess he spent less of his time in the hut, and was more frequently seen in the distant marshes of Eel River and on the upland hills. A feverish restlessness, quite opposed to his usual phlegm, led him into singular freaks strangely inconsistent with his usual habits and reputation. The purser of the occasional steamer which stopped at Logport with the mails reported to have been boarded, just inside the bar, by a strange bearded man, who asked for a newspaper containing the last war telegrams. He tore his red shirt into narrow strips, and spent two days with his needle over the pieces and the tattered remnant of his only white garment; and a few days afterward the fishermen on the bay were surprised to see what, on nearer approach, proved to be a rude imitation of the national flag floating from a spar above the hut.

One evening, as the fog began to drift over the sand-hills, the recluse sat alone in his hut. The fire was dying unheeded on the hearth, for he had been sitting there for a long time, completely absorbed in the blurred pages of an old newspaper. Presently he arose, and, refolding it,—an operation of great care and delicacy in its tattered condition,—placed it under the blankets of his bed. He resumed his seat by the fire, but soon began drumming with his fingers on the arm of his chair. Eventually this assumed the time and accent of some air. Then he began to whistle softly and hesitatingly, as if trying to recall a forgotten tune. Finally this took shape in a rude resemblance, not unlike that which his flag bore to the national standard, to Yankee Doodle. Suddenly he stopped.

There was an unmistakable rapping at the door. The blood which had at first rushed to his face now forsook it and settled slowly around his heart. He tried to rise, but could not. Then the door was flung open, and a figure with a scarlet-lined hood and fur mantle stood on the threshold. With a mighty effort he took one stride to the door. The next moment he saw the wide mouth and white teeth of the Princess, and was greeted by a kiss that felt like a baptism.

To tear the hood and mantle from her figure in the sudden fury that seized him, and to fiercely demand the reason of this masquerade, was his only return to her greeting. "Why are you here? Did you steal these garments?" he again demanded in her guttural language, as he shook her roughly by the arm. The Princess hung her head. "Did you?" he screamed, as he reached wildly for his rifle.

"I did."

His hold relaxed, and he staggered back against the wall. The Princess began to whimper. Between her sobs, she was trying to explain that the Major and his daughter were going away, and that they wanted to send her to the Reservation; but he cut her short. "Take off those things!" The Princess tremblingly obeyed. He rolled them up, placed them in the canoe she had just left, and then leaped into the frail craft. She would have followed, but with a great oath he threw her from him, and with one stroke of his paddle swept out into the fog, and was gone.

"Jessamy," said the Major, a few days after, as he sat at dinner with his daughter, "I think I can tell you something to match the mysterious disappearance and return of your wardrobe. Your crazy friend, the recluse, has enlisted this morning in the Fourth Artillery. He's a splendid-looking animal, and there's the right stuff for a soldier in him, if I'm not mistaken. He's in earnest too, for he enlists in the regiment ordered back to Washington. Bless me, child, another goblet broken; you'll ruin the mess in glassware, at this rate!"

"Have you heard anything more of the Princess, papa?"

"Nothing, but perhaps it's as well that she has gone. These cursed settlers are at their old complaints again about what they call 'Indian depredations,' and I have just received orders from headquarters to keep the settlement clear of all vagabond aborigines. I am afraid, my dear, that a strict construction of the term would include your *protégée*."

The time for the departure of the Fourth Artillery had come. The night before was thick and foggy. At one o'clock, a shot on the ramparts called out the guard and roused the sleeping garrison. The new sentry, Private Grey, had challenged a dusky figure creeping on the glacis, and, receiving no answer, had fired. The guard sent out presently returned, bearing a lifeless figure in their arms. The new sentry's zeal, joined with an ex-frontiersman's aim, was fatal.

They laid the helpless, ragged form before the guard-house door, and then saw for the first time that it was the Princess. Presently she opened her eyes. They fell upon the agonized face of her innocent slayer, but haply without intelligence or reproach.

"Georgy!" she whispered.

"Bob!"

"All's same now. Me get plenty well soon. Me make no more fuss. Me go to Reservation."

Then she stopped, a tremor ran through her limbs, and she lay still. She had gone to the Reservation. Not that devised by the wisdom of man, but that one set apart from the foundations of the world for the wisest as well as the meanest of His creatures.

V

THE THREE STRANGERS*

THOMAS HARDY

*Reprinted from "Wessex Tales" by permission of Harper and Brothers.

Among the few features of agricultural England which retain an appearance but little modified by the lapse of centuries, may be reckoned the high, grassy, and furzy downs, coombs, or ewe-leases, as they are indifferently called, that fill a large area of certain counties in the south and south-west. If any mark of human occupation is met with hereon it usually takes the form of the solitary cottage of some shepherd.

Fifty years ago such a lonely cottage stood on such a down, and may possibly be standing there now. In spite of its loneliness, however, the spot, by actual measurement, was not more than five miles from a county town. Yet, what of that? Five miles of irregular upland, during the long inimical seasons, with their sleets, snows, rains, and mists, afford withdrawing space enough to isolate a Timon or a Nebuchadnezzar; much less, in fair weather, to please that less repellant tribe, the poets, philosophers, artists, and others who "conceive and meditate of pleasant things."

Some old earthen camp or barrow, some clump of trees, at least some starved fragment of ancient hedge, is usually taken advantage of in the erection of these forlorn dwellings. But, in the present case, such a kind of shelter had been disregarded. Higher Crowstairs, as the house was called, stood quite detached and undefended. The only reason for its precise situation seemed to be the crossing of two footpaths at right angles hard by, which may have crossed there and thus for a good five hundred years. The house was thus exposed to the elements on all sides. But, though the wind up here blew unmistakably when it did blow, and the rain hit hard whenever it fell, the various weathers of the winter season were not quite so formidable on the coomb as they were imagined to be by dwellers on low ground. The raw rimes were not so pernicious as in the hollows, and the frosts were scarcely so severe. When the shepherd and his family who tenanted the house were pitied for their sufferings from the exposure, they said that upon the whole they were less inconvenienced by "wuzzes and flames" (hoarses and phlegms) than when they had lived by the stream of a snug neighbouring valley.

The night of March 28, 182-, was precisely one of the nights that were wont to call forth these expressions of commiseration. The level rainstorm smote walls, slopes, and hedges like the clothyard shafts of Senlac and Crécy. Such sheep and outdoor animals as had no shelter stood with their buttocks to the wind; while the tails of little birds trying to roost on some scraggy thorn were blown inside out like umbrellas. The gable-end of the cottage was stained with wet, and the eaves-droppings flapped against the wall. Yet never was commiseration for the shepherd more misplaced. For that cheerful rustic was entertaining a large party in glorification of the christening of his second girl.

The guests had arrived before the rain began to fall, and they were all now assembled in the chief or living-room of the dwelling. A glance into the apartment at eight o'clock on this eventful evening would have resulted in the opinion that it was as cosy and comfortable a nook as could be wished for in boisterous weather. The calling of its inhabitant was proclaimed by a number of highly-polished sheep-crooks without stems that were hung ornamentally over the fireplace, the curl of each shining crook varying from the antiquated type engraved in the patriarchal pictures of old family Bibles to the most approved fashion of the last local sheep-fair. The room was lighted by half-a-dozen candles, having wicks only a trifle smaller than the grease which enveloped them, in candlesticks that were never used but at high-days, holy-days, and family feasts. The lights were scattered about the room, two of them standing on the chimneypiece. This position of candles was in itself significant. Candles on the chimneypiece always meant a party.

On the hearth, in front of a back-brand to give substance, blazed a fire of thorns, that crackled "like the laughter of the fool."

Nineteen persons were gathered here. Of these, five women, wearing gowns of various bright hues, sat in chairs along the wall; girls shy and not shy filled the window-bench; four men, including Charley Jake the hedge-carpenter, Elijah New the parish-clerk, and John Pitcher, a neighbouring dairyman, the shepherd's father-in-law, lolled in the settle; a young man and maid, who were blushing over tentative *pourparlers* on a life-companionship, sat beneath the corner-cupboard; and an elderly engaged man of fifty or upward moved restlessly about from spots where his betrothed was not to the spot where she was. Enjoyment was pretty general, and so much the more prevailed in being unhampered by conventional restrictions. Absolute confidence in each other's good opinion begat perfect ease, while the finishing stroke of manner, amounting to a truly princely serenity, was lent to the majority by the absence of any expression or trait denoting that they wished to get on in the world, enlarge their minds, or do any eclipsing thing whatever—which nowadays so generally nips the bloom and bonhomie of all except the two extremes of the social scale.

Shepherd Fennel had married well, his wife being a dairyman's daughter from the valley below, who brought fifty guineas in her pocket—and kept them there, till they should be required for ministering to the needs of a coming family. This frugal woman had been somewhat exercised as to the character that should be given to the gathering. A sit-still party had its advantages; but an undisturbed position of ease in chairs and settles was apt to lead on the men to such an unconscionable deal of toping that they would sometimes fairly drink the house dry. A dancing-party was the alternative; but this, while avoiding the foregoing objection on the score of good drink, had a counterbalancing disadvantage in the matter of good victuals, the ravenous appetites engendered by the exercise causing immense havoc in the buttery. Shepherdess Fennel fell back upon the intermediate plan of mingling short dances with short periods of talk and singing, so as to hinder any ungovernable rage in either. But this scheme was entirely confined to her own gentle mind: the shepherd himself was in the mood to exhibit the most reckless phases of hospitality.

The fiddler was a boy of those parts, about twelve years of age, who had a wonderful dexterity in jigs and reels, though his fingers were so small and short as to necessitate a constant shifting for the high notes, from which he scrambled back to the first position with sounds not of unmixed purity of tone. At seven the shrill tweedle-dee of this youngster had begun, accompanied by a booming ground-bass from Elijah New, the parish-clerk, who had thoughtfully brought with him his favourite musical instrument, the serpent. Dancing was instantaneous, Mrs. Fennel privately enjoining the players on no account to let the dance exceed the length of a quarter of an hour.

But Elijah and the boy, in the excitement of their position, quite forgot the injunction. Moreover, Oliver Giles, a man of seventeen, one of the dancers, who was enamoured of his partner, a fair girl of thirty-three rolling years, had recklessly handed a new crown-piece to the musicians, as a bribe to keep going as long as they had muscle and wind. Mrs. Fennel, seeing the steam begin to generate on the countenances of her guests, crossed over and touched the fiddler's elbow and put her hand on the serpent's mouth. But they took no notice, and fearing she might lose her character of genial hostess if she were to interfere too markedly, she retired and sat down helpless. And so the dance whizzed on with cumulative fury, the performers moving in their planet-like courses, direct and retrograde, from apogee to perigee, till the hand of the well-kicked clock at the bottom of the room had travelled over the circumference of an hour.

While those cheerful events were in course of enactment within Fennel's pastoral dwelling, an incident having considerable bearing on the party had occurred in the gloomy night without. Mrs. Fennel's concern about the growing fierceness of the dance corresponded in point of time with the ascent of a human figure to the solitary hill of Higher Crowstairs from the direction of the distant town. This personage strode on through the rain without a pause, following the little-worn path which, further on in its course, skirted the shepherd's cottage.

It was nearly the time of full moon, and on this account, though the sky was lined with a uniform sheet of dripping cloud, ordinary objects out-of-doors were readily visible. The sad wan light revealed the lonely pedestrian to be a man of supple frame; his gait suggested that he had somewhat passed the period of perfect and instinctive agility, though not so far as to be otherwise than rapid of motion when occasion required. In point of fact he might have been about forty years of age. He appeared tall, but a recruiting sergeant, or other person accustomed to the judging of men's heights by the eye, would have discerned that this was chiefly owing to his gauntness, and that he was not more than five feet eight or nine.

Notwithstanding the regularity of his tread, there was caution in it, as in that of one who mentally feels his way; and despite the fact that it was not a black coat nor a dark garment of any sort that he wore, there was something about him which suggested that he naturally belonged to the black-coated tribes of men. His clothes were of fustian, and his boots hobnailed, yet in his progress he showed not the mud-accustomed bearing of hobnailed and fustianed peasantry.

By the time that he had arrived abreast of the shepherd's premises the rain came down, or rather came along, with yet more determined violence. The outskirts of the little homestead partially broke the force of wind and rain, and this induced him to stand still. The most salient of the shepherd's domestic erections was an empty sty at the forward corner of his hedgeless garden, for in these latitudes the principle of masking the homelier features of your establishment by a conventional frontage was unknown. The traveller's eye was attracted to this small building by the pallid shine of the wet slates that covered it. He turned aside, and, finding it empty, stood under the pent-roof for shelter.

While he stood, the boom of the serpent within, and the lesser strains of the fiddler, reached the spot as an accompaniment to the surging hiss of the flying rain on the sod, its louder beating on the cabbage-leaves of the garden, on the eight or ten beehives just discernible by the path, and its dripping from the eaves into a row of buckets and pans that had been placed under the walls of the cottage. For at Higher Crowstairs, as at all such elevated domiciles, the grand difficulty of housekeeping was an insufficiency of water; and a casual rainfall was utilized by turning out, as catchers, every utensil that the house contained. Some queer stories might be told of the contrivances for economy in suds and dish-waters that are absolutely necessitated in upland habitations during the droughts of summer. But at this season there were no such exigencies: a mere acceptance of what the skies bestowed was sufficient for an abundant store.

At last the notes of the serpent ceased and the house was silent. This cessation of activity aroused the solitary pedestrian from the reverie into which he had lapsed, and, emerging from the shed, with an apparently new intention, he walked up the path to the house-door. Arrived here, his first act was to kneel down on a large stone beside the row of vessels, and to drink a copious draught from one of them. Having quenched his thirst, he rose and lifted his hand to knock, but paused with his eye upon the panel. Since the dark surface of the wood revealed absolutely nothing, it was evident that he must be mentally looking through the door, as if he wished to measure thereby all the possibilities that a house of this sort might include, and how they might bear upon the question of his entry.

In his indecision he turned and surveyed the scene around. Not a soul was anywhere visible. The garden-path stretched downward from his feet, gleaming like the track of a snail; the roof of the little well (mostly dry), the well cover, the top rail of the garden-gate, were varnished with the same dull liquid glaze; while, far away in the vale, a faint whiteness of more than usual extent showed that the rivers were high in the meads. Beyond all this winked a few bleared lamplights through the beating drops, lights that denoted the situation of the county-town from which he had appeared to come. The absence of all notes of life in that direction seemed to clinch his intentions, and he knocked at the door.

Within, a desultory chat had taken the place of movement and musical sound. The hedge-carpenter was suggesting a song to the company, which nobody just then was inclined to undertake, so that the knock afforded a not unwelcome diversion.

"Walk in!" said the shepherd promptly.

The latch clicked upward, and out of the night our pedestrian appeared upon the door-mat. The shepherd arose, snuffed two of the nearest candles, and turned to look at him.

Their light disclosed that the stranger was dark in complexion, and not unprepossessing as to feature. His hat, which for a moment he did not remove, hung low over his eyes, without concealing that they were large, open, and determined, moving with a flash rather than a glance round the room. He seemed pleased with the survey, and, baring his shaggy head, said, in a rich deep voice, "The rain is so heavy, friends, that I ask leave to come in and rest awhile."

"To be sure, stranger," said the shepherd. "And faith, you've been lucky in choosing your time, for we are having a bit of a fling for a glad cause—though to be sure a man could hardly wish that glad cause to happen more than once a year."

"Nor less," spoke up a woman. "For 'tis best to get your family over and done with, as soon as you can, so as to be all the earlier out of the fag o't."

"And what may be this glad cause?" asked the stranger.

"A birth and christening," said the shepherd.

The stranger hoped his host might not be made unhappy either by too many or too few of such episodes, and being invited by a gesture to a pull at the mug, he readily acquiesced. His manner, which before entering had been so dubious, was now altogether that of a careless and candid man.

"Late to be traipsing athwart this coomb—hey?" said the engaged man of fifty.

"Late it is, master, as you say.—I'll take a seat in the chimney-corner, if you have nothing to urge against it, ma'am; for I am a little moist on the side that was next the rain."

Mrs. Shepherd Fennel assented, and made room for the self-invited comer, who, having got completely inside the chimney-corner, stretched out his legs and his arms with the expansiveness of a person quite at home.

"Yes, I am rather thin in the vamp," he said freely, seeing that the eyes of Shepherd's wife fell upon his boots, "and I am not well-fitted, either. I have had some rough times lately, and have been forced to pick up what I can get in the way of wearing, but I must find a suit better fit for working-days when I reach home."

"One of hereabouts?" she inquired.

"Not quite that—further up the country."

"I thought so. And so am I; and by your tongue you come from my neighbourhood."

"But you would hardly have heard of me," he said quickly. "My time would be long before yours, ma'am, you see."

This testimony to the youthfulness of his hostess had the effect of stopping her cross-examination.

"There is only one thing more wanted to make me happy," continued the newcomer. "And that is a little baccy, which I am sorry to say I am out of."

"I'll fill your pipe," said the shepherd.

"I must ask you to lend me a pipe likewise."

"A smoker, and no pipe about ye?"

"I have dropped it somewhere on the road."

The shepherd filled and handed him a new clay pipe, saying, as he did so, "Hand me your baccy-box—I'll fill that too, now I am about it."

The man went through the movement of searching his pockets.

"Lost that too?" said his entertainer, with some surprise.

"I am afraid so," said the man with some confusion. "Give it to me in a screw of paper." Lighting his pipe at the candle with a suction that drew the whole flame into the bowl, he resettled himself in the corner, and bent his looks upon the faint steam from his damp legs, as if he wished to say no more.

Meanwhile the general body of guests had been taking little notice of this visitor by reason of an absorbing discussion in which they were engaged with the band about a time for the next dance. The matter being settled, they were about to stand up when an interruption came in the shape of another knock at the door.

At sound of the same the man in the chimney-corner took up the poker and began stirring the fire as if doing it thoroughly were the one aim of his existence; and a second time the shepherd said "Walk in!" In a moment another man stood upon the straw-woven door-mat. He too was a stranger.

This individual was one of a type radically different from the first. There was more of the commonplace in his manner, and a certain jovial cosmopolitanism sat upon his features. He was several years older than the first arrival, his hair being slightly frosted, his eyebrows bristly, and his whiskers cut back from his cheeks. His face was rather full and flabby, and yet it was not altogether a face without power. A few grog-blossoms marked the neighbourhood of his nose. He flung back his long drab greatcoat, revealing that beneath it he wore a suit of cinder-grey shade throughout, large heavy seals, of some metal or other that would take a polish, dangling from his fob as his only personal ornament. Shaking the water-drops from his low-crowned glazed hat, he said, "I must ask for a few minutes' shelter, comrades, or I shall be wetted to my skin before I get to Casterbridge."

"Make yerself at home, master," said the shepherd, perhaps a trifle less heartily than on the first occasion. Not that Fennel had the least tinge of niggardliness in his composition; but the room was far from large, spare chairs were not numerous, and damp companions were not altogether comfortable at close quarters for the women and girls in their bright-coloured gowns.

However, the second comer, after taking off his greatcoat, and hanging his hat on a nail in one of the ceiling-beams as if he had been specially invited to put it there, advanced and sat down at the table. This had been pushed so closely into the chimney-corner, to give all available room to the dancers, that its inner edge grazed the elbow of the man who had ensconced himself by the fire; and thus the two strangers were brought into close companionship. They nodded to each other by way of breaking the ice of unacquaintance, and the first stranger handed his neighbour the large mug—a huge vessel of brown ware, having its upper edge worn away like a threshold by the rub of whole genealogies of thirsty lips that had gone the way of all flesh, and bearing the following inscription burnt upon its rotund side in yellow letters:—

THERE iS NO FUN
UNTiLL i CUM.

The other man, nothing loth, raised the mug to his lips, and drank on, and on, and on—till a curious blueness overspread the countenance of the shepherd's wife, who had regarded with no little surprise the first stranger's free offer to the second of what did not belong to him to dispense.

"I knew it!" said the toper to the shepherd with much satisfaction. "When I walked up your garden afore coming in, and saw the hives all of a row, I said to myself, 'Where there's bees there's honey, and where there's honey there's mead.' But mead of such a truly comfortable sort as this I really didn't expect to meet in my older days." He took yet another pull at the mug, till it assumed an ominous horizontality.

"Glad you enjoy it!" said the shepherd warmly.

"It is goodish mead," assented Mrs. Fennel with an absence of enthusiasm, which seemed to say that it was possible to buy praise for one's cellar at too heavy a price. "It is trouble enough to make—and really I hardly think we shall make any more. For honey sells well, and we can make shift with a drop o' small mead and metheglin for common use from the comb-washings."

"Oh, but you'll never have the heart!" reproachfully cried the stranger in cinder-grey, after taking up the mug a third time and setting it down empty.

"I love mead, when 'tis old like this, as I love to go to church o' Sundays, or to relieve the needy any day of the week."

"Ha, ha, ha!" said the man in the chimney-corner, who, in spite of the taciturnity induced by the pipe of tobacco, could not or would not refrain from this slight testimony to his comrade's humour.

Now the old mead of those days, brewed of the purest first-year or maiden honey, four pounds to the gallon—with its due complement of whites of eggs, cinnamon, ginger, cloves, mace, rosemary, yeast, and processes of working, bottling, and cellaring—tasted remarkably strong; but it did not taste so strong as it actually was. Hence, presently, the stranger in cinder-grey at the table, moved by its creeping influence, unbuttoned his waistcoat, threw himself back in his chair, spread his legs, and made his presence felt in various ways.

"Well, well, as I say," he resumed, "I am going to Casterbridge, and to Casterbridge I must go. I should have been almost there by this time, but the rain drove me into ye; and I'm not sorry for it."

"You don't live in Casterbridge?" said the shepherd.

"Not as yet; though I shortly mean to move there."

"Going to set up in trade, perhaps?"

"No, no," said the shepherd's wife. "It is easy to see that the gentleman is rich, and don't want to work at anything."

The cinder-gray stranger paused, as if to consider whether he would accept that definition of himself. He presently rejected it by answering, "Rich is not quite the word for me, dame. I do work, and I must work. And even if I only get to Casterbridge by midnight I must begin work there at eight tomorrow morning. Yes, het or wet, blow or snow, famine or sword, my day's work to-morrow must be done."

"Poor man! Then, in spite o' seeming, you be worse off than we?" replied the shepherd's wife.

"'Tis the nature of my trade, men and maidens. 'Tis the nature of my trade more than my poverty.... But really and truly I must up and off, or I shan't get a lodging in the town." However, the speaker did not move, and directly added, "There's time for one more draught of friendship before I go; and I'd perform it at once if the mug were not dry."

"Here's a mug o' small," said Mrs. Fennel. "Small, we call it, though to be sure 'tis only the first wash o' the combs."

"No," said the stranger disdainfully. "I won't spoil your first kindness by partaking o' your second."

"Certainly not," broke in Fennel. "We don't increase and multiply every day, and I'll fill the mug again." He went away to the dark place under the stairs where the barrel stood. The shepherdess followed him.

"Why should you do this?" she said reproachfully, as soon as they were alone. "He's emptied it once, though it held enough for ten people; and now he's not contented wi' the small, but must needs call for more o' the strong! And a stranger unbeknown to any of us. For my part I don't like the look o' the man at all."

"But he's in the house, my honey; and 'tis a wet night, and a christening. Daze it, what's a cup of mead more or less? there'll be plenty more next bee-burning."

"Very well—this time, then," she answered, looking wistfully at the barrel. "But what is the man's calling, and where is he one of, that he should come in and join us like this?"

"I don't know. I'll ask him again."

The catastrophe of having the mug drained dry at one pull by the stranger in cinder-grey was effectually guarded against this time by Mrs. Fennel. She poured out his allowance in a small cup, keeping the large one at a discreet distance from him. When he had tossed off his portion the shepherd renewed his inquiry about the stranger's occupation.

The latter did not immediately reply, and the man in the chimney-corner, with sudden demonstrativeness, said, "Anybody may know my trade—I'm a wheelwright."

"A very good trade for these parts," said the shepherd.

"And anybody may know mine—if they've the sense to find it out," said the stranger in cinder-grey.

"You may generally tell what a man is by his claws," observed the hedge-carpenter, looking at his hands. "My fingers be as full of thorns as an old pincushion is of pins."

The hands of the man in the chimney-corner instinctively sought the shade, and he gazed into the fire as he resumed his pipe. The man at the table took up the hedge-carpenter's remark, and added smartly, "True; but the oddity of my trade is that, instead of setting a mark upon me, it sets a mark upon my customers."

No observation being offered by anybody in elucidation of this enigma, the shepherd's wife once more called for a song. The same obstacles presented themselves as at the former time—one had no voice, another had forgotten the first verse. The stranger at the table, whose soul had now risen to a good working temperature, relieved the difficulty by exclaiming that, to start the company, he would sing himself. Thrusting one thumb into the arm-hole of his waistcoat, he waved the other hand in the air, and, with an extemporizing gaze at the shining sheep-crooks above the mantelpiece, began:

Oh my trade it is the rarest one,
Simple shepherds all—
My trade is a sight to see;
For my customers I tie, and take them up on high,
And waft 'em to a far countree.

The room was silent when he had finished the verse—with one exception, that of the man in the chimney-corner, who, at the singer's word, "Chorus!" joined him in a deep bass voice of musical relish—

And waft 'em to a far countree.

Oliver Giles, John Pitcher the dairyman, the parish-clerk, the engaged man of fifty, the row of young women against the wall seemed lost in thought not of the gayest kind. The shepherd looked meditatively on the ground, the shepherdess gazed keenly at the singer, and with some suspicion; she was doubting whether this stranger were merely singing an old song from recollection or was composing one there and then for the occasion. All were as perplexed at the obscure revelation as the guests at Belshazzar's Feast, except the man in the chimney-corner, who quietly said, "Second verse, stranger," and smoked on.

The singer thoroughly moistened himself from his lips inward, and went on with the next stanza as requested:—

My tools are but common ones,
Simple shepherds all,
My tools are no sight to see:
A little hempen string, and a post whereon to swing,
Are implements enough for me.

Shepherd Fennel glanced round. There was no longer any doubt that the stranger was answering his question rhythmically. The guests one and all started back with suppressed exclamations. The young woman engaged to the man of fifty fainted half-way, and would have proceeded, but finding him wanting in alacrity for catching her she sat down trembling.

"Oh, he's the—!" whispered the people in the background, mentioning the name of an ominous public officer. "He's come to do it. 'Tis to be at Casterbridge gaol to-morrow—the man for sheep-stealing—the poor clock-maker we heard of, who used to live away at Anglebury and had no work to do—Timothy Sommers, whose family were a-starving, and so he went out of Anglebury by the highroad, and took a sheep in open daylight, defying the farmer and the farmer's wife and the farmer's man, and every man jack among 'em. He" (and they nodded toward the stranger of the terrible trade) "is come from up the country to do it because there's not enough to do in his own county-town, and he's got the place here now our own county man's dead; he's going to live in the same cottage under the prison wall."

The stranger in cinder-grey took no notice of this whispered string of observations, but again wetted his lips. Seeing that his friend in the chimney-corner was the only one who reciprocated his joviality in any way, he held out his cup toward that appreciative comrade, who also held out his own. They clinked together, the eyes of the rest of the room hanging upon the singer's actions. He parted his lips for the third verse; but at that moment another knock was audible upon the door. This time the knock was faint and hesitating.

The company seemed scared; the shepherd looked with consternation toward the entrance, and it was with some effort that he resisted his alarmed wife's deprecatory glance, and uttered for the third time the welcoming words, "Walk in!"

The door was gently opened, and another man stood upon the mat. He, like those who had preceded him, was a stranger. This time it was a short, small personage, of fair complexion, and dressed in a decent suit of dark clothes.

"Can you tell me the way to—?" he began; when, gazing round the room to observe the nature of the company amongst whom he had fallen, his eyes lighted on the stranger in cinder-grey. It was just at the instant when the latter, who had thrown his mind into his song with such a will that he scarcely heeded the interruption, silenced all whispers and inquiries by bursting into his third verse:—

To-morrow is my working day,
Simple shepherds all—
To-morrow is a working day for me:
For the farmer's sheep is slain, and the lad who did it ta'en,
And on his soul may God ha' merc-y!

The stranger in the chimney-corner, waving cups with the singer so heartily that his mead splashed over on the hearth, repeated in his bass voice as before:—

And on his soul may God ha' merc-y!

All this time the third stranger had been standing in the doorway. Finding now that he did not come forward or go on speaking, the guests particularly regarded him. They noticed to their surprise that he stood before them the picture of abject terror—his knees trembling, his hand shaking so violently that the door-latch by which he supported himself rattled audibly; his white lips were parted, and his eyes fixed on the merry officer of justice in the middle of the room. A moment more and he had turned, closed the door, and fled.

"What a man can it be?" said the shepherd.

The rest, between the awfulness of their late discovery and the odd conduct of this third visitor, looked as if they knew not what to think, and said nothing. Instinctively they withdrew further and further from the grim gentleman in their midst, whom some of them seemed to take for the Prince of Darkness himself, till they formed a remote circle, an empty space of floor being left between them and him—

——circulus, cujus centrum diabolus.

The room was so silent—though there were more than twenty people in it—that nothing could be heard but the patter of the rain against the window-shutters, accompanied by the occasional hiss of a stray drop that fell down the chimney into the fire, and the steady puffing of the man in the corner, who had now resumed his pipe of long clay.

The stillness was unexpectedly broken. The distant sound of a gun reverberated through the air—apparently from the direction of the county-town.

"Be jiggered!" cried the stranger who had sung the song, jumping up.

"What does that mean?" asked several.

"A prisoner escaped from the gaol—that's what it means."

All listened. The sound was repeated, and none of them spoke but the man in the chimney-corner, who said quietly, "I've often been told that in this county they fire a gun at such times; but I never heard it till now."

"I wonder if it is my man?" murmured the personage in cinder-grey.

"Surely it is!" said the shepherd involuntarily. "And surely we've seen him! That little man who looked in at the door by now, and quivered like a leaf when he seed ye and heard your song!"

"His teeth chattered, and the breath went out of his body," said the dairyman.

"And his heart seemed to sink within him like a stone," said Oliver Giles.

"And he bolted as if he'd been shot at," said the hedge-carpenter.

"True—his teeth chattered, and his heart seemed to sink; and he bolted as if he'd been shot at," slowly summed up the man in the chimney-corner.

"I didn't notice it," remarked the grim songster.

"We were all a-wondering what made him run off in such a fright," faltered one of the women against the wall, "and now 'tis explained."

The firing of the alarm-gun went on at intervals, low and sullenly, and their suspicions became a certainty. The sinister gentleman in cinder-grey roused himself. "Is there a constable here?" he asked in thick tones. "If so, let him step forward."

The engaged man of fifty stepped quavering out of the corner, his betrothed beginning to sob on the back of the chair.

"You are a sworn constable?"

"I be, sir."

"Then pursue the criminal at once, with assistance, and bring him back here. He can't have gone far."

"I will, sir, I will—when I've got my staff. I'll go home and get it, and come sharp here, and start in a body."

"Staff!—never mind your staff; the man'll be gone!"

"But I can't do nothing without my staff—can I, William, and John, and Charles Jake? No; for there's the king's royal crown a painted on en in yaller and gold, and the lion and the unicorn, so as when I raise en up and hit my prisoner, 'tis made a lawful blow thereby. I wouldn't 'tempt to take up a man without my staff—no, not I. If I hadn't the law to gie me courage, why, instead o' my taking up him he might take up me!"

"Now, I'm a king's man myself, and can give you authority enough for this," said the formidable person in cinder-grey. "Now then, all of ye, be ready. Have ye any lanterns?"

"Yes—have ye any lanterns?—I demand it," said the constable.

"And the rest of you able-bodied——"

"Able-bodied men—yes—the rest of ye," said the constable.

"Have you some good stout staves and pitchforks——"

"Staves and pitchforks—in the name o' the law. And take 'em in yer hands and go in quest, and do as we in authority tell ye."

Thus aroused, the men prepared to give chase. The evidence was, indeed, though circumstantial, so convincing, that but little argument was needed to show the shepherd's guests that after what they had seen it would look very much like connivance if they did not instantly pursue the unhappy third stranger, who could not as yet have gone more than a few hundred yards over such uneven country.

A shepherd is always well provided with lanterns; and, lighting these hastily, and with hurdle-staves in their hands, they poured out of the door, taking a direction along the crest of the hill away from the town, the rain having fortunately a little abated.

Disturbed by the noise, or possibly by unpleasant dreams of her baptism, the child who had been christened began to cry heartbrokenly in the room overhead. These notes of grief came down through the chinks of the floor to the ears of the women below, who jumped up one by one, and seemed glad of the excuse to ascend and comfort the baby, for the incidents of the last half hour greatly oppressed them. Thus in the space of two or three minutes the room on the ground floor was deserted quite.

But it was not for long. Hardly had the sound of footsteps died away when a man returned round the corner of the house from the direction the pursuers had taken. Peeping in at the door, and seeing nobody there, he entered leisurely. It was the stranger of the chimney-corner, who had gone out with the rest. The motive of his return was shown by his helping himself to a cut piece of skimmer-cake that lay on a ledge beside where he had sat, and which he had apparently forgotten to take with him. He also poured out half a cup more mead from the quantity that remained, ravenously eating and drinking these as he stood. He had not finished when another figure came in just as quietly—the stranger in cinder-grey.

"Oh—you here?" said the latter smiling. "I thought you had gone to help in the capture." And this speaker also revealed the object of his return by looking solicitously round for the fascinating mug of old mead.

"And I thought you had gone," said the other, continuing his skimmer-cake with some effort.

"Well, on second thoughts, I felt there were enough without me," said the first confidentially, "and such a night as it is, too. Besides, 'tis the business o' the Government to take care of its criminals—not mine."

"True; so it is. And I felt as you did, that there were enough without me."

"I don't want to break my limbs running over the humps and hollows of this wild country."

"Nor I neither, between you and me."

"These shepherd-people are used to it—simple-minded souls, you know, stirred up to anything in a moment. They'll have him ready for me before the morning, and no trouble to me at all."

"They'll have him, and we shall have saved ourselves all labour in the matter."

"True, true. Well, my way is to Casterbridge; and 'tis as much as my legs will do to take me that far. Going the same way?"

"No, I am sorry to say. I have to get home over there" (he nodded indefinitely to the right), "and I feel as you do, that it is quite enough for my legs to do before bedtime."

The other had by this time finished the mead in the mug, after which, shaking hands at the door, and wishing each other well, they went their several ways.

In the meantime the company of pursuers had reached the end of the hog's-back elevation which dominated this part of the coomb. They had decided on no particular plan of action; and, finding that the man of the baleful trade was no longer in their company, they seemed quite unable to form any such plan now. They descended in all directions down the hill, and straightway several of the party fell into the snare set by Nature for all misguided midnight ramblers over the lower cretaceous formation. The "lynchets," or flint slopes, which belted the escarpment at intervals of a dozen yards, took the less cautious ones unawares, and losing their footing on the rubbly steep they slid sharply downward, the lanterns rolling from their hands to the bottom, and there lying on their sides till the horn was scorched through.

When they had again gathered themselves together, the shepherd, as the man who knew the country best, took the lead, and guided them round these treacherous inclines. The lanterns, which seemed rather to dazzle their eyes and warn the fugitive than to assist them in the exploration, were extinguished, due silence was observed; and in this more rational order they plunged into the vale. It was a grassy, briary, moist channel, affording some shelter to any person who had sought it; but the party perambulated it in vain, and ascended on the other side. Here they wandered apart, and after an interval closed together again to report progress. At the second time of closing in they found themselves near a lonely oak, the single tree on this part of the upland, probably sown there by a passing bird some hundred years before. And here, standing a little to one side of the trunk, as motionless as the trunk itself, appeared the man they were in quest of, his outline being well defined against the sky beyond. The band noiselessly drew up and faced him.

"Your money or your life!" said the constable sternly to the still figure.

"No, no," whispered John Pitcher. "'Tisn't our side ought to say that. That's the doctrine of vagabonds like him, and we be on the side of the law."

"Well, well," replied the constable impatiently; "I must say something, mustn't I? and if you had all the weight o' this undertaking upon your mind, perhaps you'd say the wrong thing too.—Prisoner at the bar, surrender, in the name of the Fath——the Crown, I mane!"

The man under the tree seemed now to notice them for the first time, and, giving them no opportunity whatever for exhibiting their courage, he strolled slowly toward them. He was, indeed, the little man, the third stranger; but his trepidation had in a great measure gone.

"Well, travellers," he said, "did I hear ye speak to me?"

"You did: you've got to come and be our prisoner at once," said the constable. "We arrest ye on the charge of not biding in Casterbridge gaol in a decent proper manner to be hung to-morrow morning. Neighbours, do your duty, and seize the culpet!"

On hearing the charge, the man seemed enlightened, and, saying not another word, resigned himself with preternatural civility to the search-party, who, with their staves in their hands, surrounded him on all sides, and marched him back toward the shepherd's cottage.

It was eleven o'clock by the time they arrived. The light shining from the open door, a sound of men's voices within, proclaimed to them as they approached the house that some new events had arisen in their absence. On entering they discovered the shepherd's living-room to be invaded by two officers from Casterbridge gaol, and a well-known magistrate who lived at the nearest country seat, intelligence of the escape having become generally circulated.

"Gentlemen," said the constable, "I have brought back your man—not without risk and danger; but every one must do his duty. He is inside this circle of able-bodied persons, who have lent me useful aid considering their ignorance of Crown work. Men, bring forward your prisoner." And the third stranger was led to the light.

"Who is this?" said one of the officials.

"The man," said the constable.

"Certainly not," said the other turnkey; and the first corroborated his statement.

"But how can it be otherwise?" asked the constable. "Or why was he so terrified at sight o' the singing instrument of the law?" Here he related the strange behaviour of the third stranger on entering the house.

"Can't understand it," said the officer coolly. "All I know is that it is not the condemned man. He's quite a different character from this one; a gauntish fellow, with dark hair and eyes, rather good-looking, and with a musical bass voice that if you heard it once you'd never mistake as long as you lived."

"Why, souls—'twas the man in the chimney-corner!"

"Hey—what?" said the magistrate, coming forward after inquiring particulars from the shepherd in the background. "Haven't you got the man after all?"

"Well, sir," said the constable, "he's the man we were in search of, that's true; and yet he's not the man we were in search of. For the man we were in search of was not the man we wanted, sir, if you understand my everyday way; for 'twas the man in the chimney-corner."

"A pretty kettle of fish altogether!" said the magistrate. "You had better start for the other man at once."

The prisoner now spoke for the first time. The mention of the man in the chimney-corner seemed to have moved him as nothing else could do. "Sir," he said, stepping forward to the magistrate, "take no more trouble about me. The time is come when I may as well speak. I have done nothing; my crime is that the condemned man is my brother. Early this afternoon I left home at Anglebury to tramp it all the way to Casterbridge gaol to bid him farewell. I was benighted, and called here to rest and ask the way. When I opened the door I saw before me the very man, my brother, that I thought to see in the condemned cell at Casterbridge. He was in this chimney-corner; and jammed close to him, so that he could not have got out if he had tried, was the executioner who'd come to take his life, singing a song about it and not knowing that it was his victim who was close by, joining in to save appearances. My brother looked a glance of agony at me, and I knew he meant, 'Don't reveal what you see; my life depends on it.' I was so terror-struck that I could hardly stand, and, not knowing what I did, I turned and hurried away."

The narrator's manner and tone had the stamp of truth, and his story made a great impression on all around. "And do you know where your brother is at the present time?" asked the magistrate.

"I do not. I have never seen him since I closed this door."

"I can testify to that, for we've been between ye ever since," said the constable.

"Where does he think to fly to? What is his occupation?"

"He's a watch-and-clock-maker, sir."

"'A said 'a was a wheelwright—a wicked rogue," said the constable.

"The wheels o' clocks and watches he meant, no doubt," said Shepherd Fennel. "I thought his hands were palish for's trade."

"Well, it appears to me that nothing can be gained by retaining this poor man in custody," said the magistrate; "your business lies with the other, unquestionably."

And so the little man was released off-hand; but he looked nothing the less sad on that account, it being beyond the power of magistrate or constable to raze out the written troubles in his brain, for they concerned another whom he regarded with more solicitude than himself. When this was done, and the man had gone his way, the night was found to be so far advanced that it was deemed useless to renew the search before the next morning.

Next day, accordingly, the quest for the clever sheep-stealer became general and keen, to all appearance at least. But the intended punishment was cruelly disproportioned to the transgression, and the sympathy of a great many country folk in that district was strongly on the side of the fugitive. Moreover, his marvellous coolness and daring under the unprecedented circumstances of the shepherd's party won their admiration. So that it may be questioned if all those who ostensibly made themselves so busy in exploring woods and fields and lanes were quite so thorough when it came to the private examination of their own lofts and outhouses. Stories were afloat of a mysterious figure being occasionally seen in some old overgrown trackway or other, remote from turnpike roads; but when a search was instituted in any of these suspected quarters nobody was found. Thus the days and weeks passed without tidings.

In brief, the bass-voiced man of the chimney-corner was never recaptured. Some said that he went across the sea, others that he did not, but buried himself in the depths of a populous city. At any rate, the gentleman in cinder-grey never did his morning's work at Casterbridge, nor met anywhere at all, for business purposes, the comrade with whom he had passed an hour of relaxation in the lonely house on the coomb.

The grass has long been green on the graves of Shepherd Fennel and his frugal wife; the guests who made up the christening party have mainly followed their entertainers to the tomb; the baby in whose honour they all had met is a matron in the sere and yellow leaf. But the arrival of the three strangers at the shepherd's that night, and the details connected therewith, is a story as well known as ever in the country about Higher Crowstairs.

VI

THE PASSING OF BLACK EAGLE

O. HENRY

For some months of a certain year a grim bandit infested the Texas border along the Rio Grande. Peculiarly striking to the optic nerve was this notorious marauder. His personality secured him the title of "Black Eagle, the Terror of the Border." Many fearsome tales are of record concerning the doings of him and his followers. Suddenly, in the space of a single minute, Black Eagle vanished from the earth. He was never heard of again. His own band never even guessed the mystery of his disappearance. The border ranches and settlements feared he would come again to ride and ravage the mesquite flats. He never will. It is to disclose the fate of Black Eagle that this narrative is written.

The initial movement of the story is furnished by the foot of a bartender in St. Louis. His discerning eye fell upon the form of Chicken Ruggles as he pecked with avidity at the free lunch. Chicken was a "hobo." He had a long nose like the bill of a fowl, an inordinate appetite for poultry, and a habit of gratifying it without expense, which accounts for the name given him by his fellow vagrants.

Physicians agree that the partaking of liquids at meal times is not a healthy practice. The hygiene of the saloon promulgates the opposite. Chicken had neglected to purchase a drink to accompany his meal. The bartender rounded the counter, caught the injudicious diner by the ear with a lemon squeezer, led him to the door and kicked him into the street.

Thus the mind of Chicken was brought to realize the signs of coming winter. The night was cold; the stars shone with unkindly brilliancy; people were hurrying along the streets in two egotistic, jostling streams. Men had donned their overcoats, and Chicken knew to an exact percentage the increased difficulty of coaxing dimes from those buttoned-in vest pockets. The time had come for his annual exodus to the South.

A little boy, five or six years old, stood looking with covetous eyes in a confectioner's window. In one small hand he held an empty two-ounce vial; in the other he grasped tightly something flat and round, with a shining milled edge. The scene presented a field of operations commensurate to Chicken's talents and daring. After sweeping the horizon to make sure that no official tug was cruising near, he insidiously accosted his prey. The boy, having been early taught by his household to regard altruistic advances with extreme suspicion, received the overtures coldly.

Then Chicken knew that he must make one of those desperate, nerve-shattering plunges into speculation that fortune sometimes requires of those who would win her favour. Five cents was his capital, and this he must risk against the chance of winning what lay within the close grasp of the youngster's chubby hand. It was a fearful lottery, Chicken knew. But he must accomplish his end by strategy, since he had a wholesome terror of plundering infants by force. Once, in a park, driven by hunger, he had committed an onslaught upon a bottle of peptonized infant's food in the possession of an occupant of a baby carriage. The outraged infant had so promptly opened its mouth and pressed the button that communicated with the welkin that help arrived, and Chicken did his thirty days in a snug coop. Wherefore he was, as he said, "leary of kids."

Beginning artfully to question the boy concerning his choice of sweets, he gradually drew out the information he wanted. Mamma said he was to ask the drug-store man for ten cents' worth of paregoric in the bottle; he was to keep his hand shut tight over the dollar; he must not stop to talk to anyone in the street; he must ask the drug-store man to wrap up the change and put it in the pocket of his trousers. Indeed, they had pockets—two of them! And he liked chocolates cream best.

Chicken went into the store and turned plunger. He invested his entire capital in C.A.N.D.Y. stocks, simply to pave the way to the greater risk following.

He gave the sweets to the youngster, and had the satisfaction of perceiving that confidence was established. After that it was easy to obtain leadership of the expedition, to take the investment by the hand and lead it to a nice drug store he knew of in the same block. There Chicken, with a parental air, passed over the dollar and called for the medicine, while the boy crunched his candy, glad to be relieved of the responsibility of the purchase. And then the successful investor, searching his pockets, found an overcoat button—the extent of his winter trousseau—and, wrapping it carefully, placed the ostensible change in the pocket of confiding juvenility. Setting the youngster's face homeward, and patting him benevolently on the back—for Chicken's heart was as soft as those of his feathered namesakes—the speculator quit the market with a profit of 1,700 per cent. on his invested capital.

Two hours later an Iron Mountain freight engine pulled out of the railroad yards, Texas bound, with a string of empties. In one of the cattle cars, half buried in excelsior, Chicken lay at ease. Beside him in the nest was a quart bottle of very poor whiskey and a paper bag of bread and cheese. Mr. Ruggles, in his private car, was on his trip south for the winter season.

For a week that car was trundled southward, shifted, laid over, and manipulated after the manner of rolling stock, but Chicken stuck to it, leaving it only at necessary times to satisfy his hunger and thirst. He knew it must go down to the cattle country, and San Antonio, in the heart of it, was his goal. There the air was salubrious and mild; the people indulgent and long-suffering. The bartenders there would not kick him. If he should eat too long or too often at one place they would swear at him as if by rote and without heat. They swore so drawlingly, and they rarely paused short of their full vocabulary, which was copious, so that Chicken had often gulped a good meal during the process of the vituperative prohibition. The season there was always spring-like; the plazas were pleasant at night, with music and gaiety; except during the slight and infrequent cold snaps one could sleep comfortably out-of-doors in case the interiors should develop inhospitality.

At Texarkana his car was switched to the I. and G. N. Then still southward it trailed until, at length, it crawled across the Colorado bridge at Austin, and lined out, straight as an arrow, for the run to San Antonio.

When the freight halted at that town Chicken was fast asleep. In ten minutes the train was off again for Laredo, the end of the road. Those empty cattle cars were for distribution along the line at points from which the ranches shipped their stock.

When Chicken awoke his car was stationary. Looking out between the slats he saw it was a bright, moonlit night. Scrambling out, he saw his car with three others abandoned on a little siding in a wild and lonesome country. A cattle pen and chute stood on one side of the track. The railroad bisected a vast, dim ocean of prairie, in the midst of which Chicken, with his futile rolling stock, was as completely stranded as was Robinson with his land-locked boat.

A white post stood near the rails. Going up to it, Chicken read the letters at the top, S.A.90. Laredo was nearly as far to the south. He was almost a hundred miles from any town. Coyotes began to yelp in the mysterious sea around him. Chicken felt lonesome. He had lived in Boston without an education, in Chicago without nerve, in Philadelphia without a sleeping place, in New York without a pull, and in Pittsburgh sober, and yet he had never felt so lonely as now.

Suddenly through the intense silence, he heard the whicker of a horse. The sound came from the side of the track toward the east, and Chicken began to explore timorously in that direction. He stepped high along the mat of curly mesquite grass, for he was afraid of everything there might be in this wilderness—snakes, rats, brigands, centipedes, mirages, cowboys, fandangoes, tarantulas, tamales—he had read of them in the story papers. Rounding a clump of prickly pear that reared high its fantastic and menacing array of rounded heads, he was struck to shivering terror by a snort and a thunderous plunge, as the horse, himself startled, bounded away some fifty yards, and then resumed his grazing. But here was the one thing in the desert that Chicken did not fear. He had been reared on a farm; he had handled horses, understood them, and could ride.

Approaching slowly and speaking soothingly, he followed the animal, which, after its first flight seemed gentle enough, and secured the end of the twenty-foot lariat that dragged after him in the grass. It required him but a few moments to contrive the rope into an ingenious nose-bridle, after the style of the Mexican *borsal*. In another he was upon the horse's back and off at a splendid lope, giving the animal free choice of direction. "He will take me somewhere," said Chicken to himself.

It would have been a thing of joy, that untrammelled gallop over the moonlit prairie, even to Chicken, who loathed exertion, but that his mood was not for it. His head ached; a growing thirst was upon him; the "somewhere" whither his lucky mount might convey him was full of dismal peradventure.

And now he noted that the horse moved to a definite goal. Where the prairie lay smooth he kept his course straight as an arrow's toward the east. Deflected by hill or arroyo or impracticable spinous brakes he quickly flowed again into the current, charted by his unerring instinct. At last, upon the side of a gentle rise, he suddenly subsided to a complacent walk. A stone's cast away stood a little mott of coma trees; beneath it a jacal such as the Mexicans erect—a one-room house of upright poles daubed with clay and roofed with grass or tule reeds. An experienced eye would have estimated the spot as the headquarters of a small sheep ranch. In the moonlight the ground in the nearby corral showed pulverized to a level smoothness by the hoofs of the sheep. Everywhere was carelessly distributed the paraphernalia of the place—ropes, bridles, saddles, sheep pelts, wool sacks, feed troughs and camp litter. The barrel of drinking water stood in the end of the two-horse wagon near the door. The harness was piled, promiscuous, upon the wagon tongue, soaking up the dew.

Chicken slipped to earth, and tied the horse to a tree. He halloed again and again, but the house remained quiet. The door stood open, and he entered cautiously. The light was sufficient for him to see that no one was at home. He struck a match and lighted a lamp that stood on a table. The room was that of a bachelor ranchman who was content with the necessaries of life. Chicken rummaged intelligently until he found what he had hardly dared hope for—a small, brown jug that still contained something near a quart of his desire.

Half an hour later, Chicken—now a gamecock of hostile aspect—emerged from the house with unsteady steps. He had drawn upon the absent ranchman's equipment to replace his own ragged attire. He wore a suit of coarse brown ducking, the coat being a sort of rakish bolero, jaunty to a degree. Boots he had donned, and spurs that whirred with every lurching step. Buckled around him was a belt full of cartridges with a big six-shooter in each of its two holsters.

Prowling about, he found blankets, a saddle and bridle with which he caparisoned his steed. Again mounting, he rode swiftly away, singing a loud and tuneless song.

Bud King's band of desperadoes, outlaws and horse and cattle thieves were in camp at a secluded spot on the bank of the Frio. Their depredations in the Rio Grande country, while no bolder than usual, had been advertised more extensively, and Captain Kinney's company of rangers had been ordered down to look after them. Consequently, Bud King, who was a wise general, instead of cutting out a hot trail for the upholders of the law, as his men wished to do, retired for the time to the prickly fastnesses of the Frio valley.

Though the move was a prudent one, and not incompatible with Bud's well-known courage, it raised dissension among the members of the band. In fact, while they thus lay ingloriously *perdu* in the brush, the question of Bud King's fitness for the leadership was argued, with closed doors, as it were, by his followers. Never before had Bud's skill or efficiency been brought to criticism; but his glory was waning (and such is glory's fate) in the light of a newer star. The sentiment of the band was crystallising into the opinion that Black Eagle could lead them with more lustre, profit, and distinction.

This Black Eagle—sub-titled the "Terror of the Border"—had been a member of the gang about three months.

One night while they were in camp on the San Miguel water-hole a solitary horseman on the regulation fiery steed dashed in among them. The new-comer was of a portentous and devastating aspect. A beak-like nose with a predatory curve projected above a mass of bristling, blue-black whiskers. His eye was cavernous and fierce. He was spurred, sombreroed, booted, garnished with revolvers, abundantly drunk, and very much unafraid. Few people in the country drained by the Rio Bravo would have cared thus to invade alone the camp of Bud King. But this fell bird swooped fearlessly upon them and demanded to be fed.

Hospitality in the prairie country is not limited. Even if your enemy pass your way you must feed him before you shoot him. You must empty your larder into him before you empty your lead. So the stranger of undeclared intentions was set down to a mighty feast.

A talkative bird he was, full of most marvellous loud tales and exploits, and speaking a language at times obscure but never colourless. He was a new sensation to Bud King's men, who rarely encountered new types. They hung, delighted, upon his vainglorious boasting, the spicy strangeness of his lingo, his contemptuous familiarity with life, the world, and remote places, and the extravagant frankness with which he conveyed his sentiments.

To their guest the band of outlaws seemed to be nothing more than a congregation of country bumpkins whom he was "stringing for grub" just as he would have told his stories at the back door of a farmhouse to wheedle a meal. And, indeed, his ignorance was not without excuse, for the "bad man" of the Southwest does not run to extremes. Those brigands might justly have been taken for a little party of peaceable rustics assembled for a fish-fry or pecan gathering. Gentle of manner, slouching of gait, soft-voiced, unpicturesquely clothed; not one of them presented to the eye any witness of the desperate records they had earned.

For two days the glittering stranger within the camp was feasted. Then, by common consent, he was invited to become a member of the band. He consented, presenting for enrollment the prodigious name of "Captain Montressor." This name was immediately overruled by the band, and "Piggy" substituted as a compliment to the awful and insatiate appetite of its owner.

Thus did the Texas border receive the most spectacular brigand that ever rode its chaparral.

For the next three months Bud King conducted business as usual, escaping encounters with law officers and being content with reasonable profits. The band ran off some very good companies of horses from the ranges, and a few bunches of fine cattle which they got safely across the Rio Grande and disposed of to fair advantage. Often the band would ride into the little villages and Mexican settlements, terrorising the inhabitants and plundering for the provisions and ammunition they needed. It was during these bloodless raids that Piggy's ferocious aspect and frightful voice gained him a renown more widespread and glorious than those other gentle-voiced and sad-faced desperadoes could have acquired in a lifetime.

The Mexicans, most apt in nomenclature, first called him The Black Eagle, and used to frighten the babes by threatening them with tales of the dreadful robber who carried off little children in his great beak. Soon the name extended, and Black Eagle, the Terror of the Border, became a recognized factor in exaggerated newspaper reports and ranch gossip.

The country from the Nueces to the Rio Grande was a wild but fertile stretch, given over to the sheep and cattle ranches. Range was free; the inhabitants were few; the law was mainly a letter and the pirates met with little opposition until the flaunting and garish Piggy gave the band undue advertisement. Then McKinney's ranger company headed for those precincts, and Bud King knew that it meant grim and sudden war or else temporary retirement. Regarding the risk to be unnecessary, he drew off his band to an almost inaccessible spot on the bank of the Frio. Wherefore, as has been said, dissatisfaction arose among the members, and impeachment proceedings against Bud were premeditated, with Black Eagle in high favour for the succession. Bud King was not unaware of the sentiment, and he called aside Cactus Taylor, his trusted lieutenant, to discuss it.

"If the boys," said Bud, "ain't satisfied with me, I'm willin' to step out. They're buckin' against my way of handlin' 'em. And 'specially because I concludes to hit the brush while Sam Kinney is ridin' the line. I saves 'em from bein' shot or sent up on a state contract, and they up and says I'm no good."

"It ain't so much that," explained Cactus, "as it is they're plum locoed about Piggy. They want them whiskers and that nose of his to split the wind at the head of the column."

"There's somethin' mighty seldom about Piggy," declared Bud, musingly. "I never yet see anything on the hoof that he exactly grades up with. He can shore holler a plenty, and he straddles a hoss from where you laid the chunk. But he ain't never been smoked yet. You know, Cactus, we ain't had a row since he's been with us. Piggy's all right for skearin' the greaser kids and layin' waste a crossroads store. I reckon he's the finest canned oyster buccaneer and cheese pirate that ever was, but how's his appetite for fightin'? I've knowed some citizens you'd think was starvin' for trouble get a bad case of dyspepsy the first dose of lead they had to take."

"He talks all spraddled out," said Cactus, "'bout the rookuses he's been in. He claims to have saw the elephant and hearn the owl."

"I know," replied Bud, using the cowpuncher's expressive phrase of skepticism, "but it sounds to me!"

This conversation was held one night in camp while the other members of the band—eight in number—were sprawling around the fire, lingering over their supper. When Bud and Cactus ceased talking they heard Piggy's formidable voice holding forth to the others as usual while he was engaged in checking, though never satisfying, his ravening appetite.

"Wat's de use," he was saying, "of chasin' little red cowses and hosses 'round for t'ousands of miles? Dere ain't nuttin' in it. Gallopin' t'rough dese bushes and briers, and gettin' a t'irst dat a brewery couldn't put out, and missin' meals! Say! You know what I'd do if I was main finger of dis bunch? I'd stick up a train. I'd blow de express car and make hard dollars where you guys gets wind. Youse makes me tired. Dis sook-cow kind of cheap sport gives me a pain."

Later on, a deputation waited on Bud. They stood on one leg, chewed mesquit twigs and circumlocuted, for they hated to hurt his feelings. Bud foresaw their business, and made it easy for them. Bigger risks and larger profits was what they wanted.

The suggestion of Piggy's about holding up a train had fired their imagination and increased their admiration for the dash and boldness of the instigator. They were such simple, artless, and custom-bound bush-rangers that they had never before thought of extending their habits beyond the running off of live-stock and the shooting of such of their acquaintances as ventured to interfere.

Bud acted "on the level," agreeing to take a subordinate place in the gang until Black Eagle should have been given a trial as leader.

After a great deal of consultation, studying of time-tables, and discussion of the country's topography, the time and place for carrying out their new enterprise was decided upon. At that time there was a feedstuff famine in Mexico and a cattle famine in certain parts of the United States, and there was a brisk international trade. Much money was being shipped along the railroads that connected the two republics. It was agreed that the most promising place for the contemplated robbery was at Espina, a little station on the I. and G. N., about forty miles north of Laredo. The train stopped there one minute; the country around was wild and unsettled; the station consisted of but one house in which the agent lived.

Black Eagle's band set out, riding by night. Arriving in the vicinity of Espina they rested their horses all day in a thicket a few miles distant.

The train was due at Espina at 10.30 P.M. They could rob the train and be well over the Mexican border with their booty by daylight the next morning.

To do Black Eagle justice, he exhibited no signs of flinching from the responsible honours that had been conferred upon him.

He assigned his men to their respective posts with discretion, and coached them carefully as to their duties. On each side of the track four of the band were to lie concealed in the chaparral. Gotch-Ear Rodgers was to stick up the station agent. Bronco Charlie was to remain with the horses, holding them in readiness. At a spot where it was calculated the engine would be when the train stopped, Bud King was to lie hidden on one side, and Black Eagle himself on the other. The two would get the drop on the engineer and fireman, force them to descend and proceed to the rear. Then the express car would be looted, and the escape made. No one was to move until Black Eagle gave the signal by firing his revolver. The plan was perfect.

At ten minutes to train time every man was at his post, effectually concealed by the thick chaparral that grew almost to the rails. The night was dark and lowering, with a fine drizzle falling from the flying gulf clouds. Black Eagle crouched behind a bush within five yards of the track. Two six-shooters were belted around him. Occasionally he drew a large black bottle from his pocket and raised it to his mouth.

A star appeared far down the track which soon waxed into the headlight of the approaching train. It came on with an increasing roar; the engine bore down upon the ambushing desperadoes with a glare and a shriek like some avenging monster come to deliver them to justice. Black Eagle flattened himself upon the ground. The engine, contrary to their calculations, instead of stopping between him and Bud King's place of concealment, passed fully forty yards farther before it came to a stand.

The bandit leader rose to his feet and peered around the bush. His men all lay quiet, awaiting the signal. Immediately opposite Black Eagle was a thing that drew his attention. Instead of being a regular passenger train it was a mixed one. Before him stood a box car, the door of which, by some means, had been left slightly open. Black Eagle went up to it and pushed the door farther open. An odour came forth—a damp, rancid, familiar, musty, intoxicating, beloved odour stirring strongly at old memories of happy days and travels. Black Eagle sniffed at the witching smell as the returned wanderer smells of the rose that twines his boyhood's cottage home. Nostalgia seized him. He put his hand inside. Excelsior—dry, springy, curly, soft, enticing, covered the floor. Outside the drizzle had turned to a chilling rain.

The train bell clanged. The bandit chief unbuckled his belt and cast it, with its revolvers, upon the ground. His spurs followed quickly, and his broad sombrero. Black Eagle was moulting. The train started with a rattling jerk. The ex-Terror of the Border scrambled into the box car and closed the door. Stretched luxuriously upon the excelsior, with the black bottle clasped closely to his breast, his eyes closed, and a foolish, happy smile upon his terrible features Chicken Ruggles started upon his return trip.

Undisturbed, with the band of desperate bandits lying motionless, awaiting the signal to attack, the train pulled out from Espina. As its speed increased, and the black masses of chaparral went whizzing past on either side, the express messenger, lighting his pipe, looked through his window and remarked, feelingly:

"What a jim-dandy place for a hold-up!"

VII

NIÑO DIABLO*

W. H. HUDSON

*Reprinted from the volume, Tales of the Pampas, by permission of Alfred A. Knopf, Inc.

The wide pampas rough with long grass; a vast level disc now growing dark, the horizon encircling it with a ring as faultless as that made by a pebble dropped into smooth water; above it the clear sky of June, wintry and pale, still showing in the west the saffron hues of the afterglow tinged with vapoury violet and grey. In the centre of the disc a large low rancho thatched with yellow rushes, a few stunted trees and cattle enclosures grouped about it; and dimly seen in the shadows, cattle and sheep reposing. At the gate stands Gregory Gorostiaga, lord of house, lands and ruminating herds, leisurely unsaddling his horse; for whatsoever Gregory does is done leisurely. Although no person is within earshot he talks much over his task, now rebuking his restive animal, and now cursing his benumbed fingers and the hard knots in his gear. A curse falls readily and not without a certain natural grace from Gregory's lips; it is the oiled feather with which he touches every difficult knot encountered in life. From time to time he glances toward the open kitchen door, from which issue the far-flaring light of the fire and familiar voices, with savoury smells of cookery that come to his nostrils like pleasant messengers.

The unsaddling over at last the freed horse gallops away, neighing joyfully, to seek his fellows; but Gregory is not a four-footed thing to hurry himself; and so, stepping slowly and pausing frequently to look about him as if reluctant to quit the cold night air, he turns toward the house.

The spacious kitchen was lighted by two or three wicks in cups of melted fat, and by a great fire in the middle of the clay floor that cast crowds of dancing shadows on the walls and filled the whole room with grateful warmth. On the walls were fastened many deers' heads, and on their convenient prongs were hung bridles and lassos, ropes of onions and garlic, bunches of dried herbs, and various other objects. At the fire a piece of beef was roasting on a spit; and in a large pot suspended by hook and chain from the smoke-blackened central beam, boiled and bubbled an ocean of mutton broth, puffing out white clouds of steam redolent of herbs and cummin-seed. Close to the fire, skimmer in hand, sat Magdalen, Gregory's fat and florid wife, engaged in frying pies in a second smaller pot. There also, on a high, straight-backed chair, sat Ascension, her sister-in-law, a wrinkled spinster; also, in a low rush-bottomed seat, her mother-in-law, an ancient white-headed dame, staring vacantly into the flames. On the other side of the fire were Gregory's two eldest daughters, occupied just now in serving *maté* to their elders—that harmless bitter decoction the sipping of which fills up all vacant moments from dawn to bed-time—pretty dove-eyed girls of sixteen, both also named Magdalen, but not after their mother nor because confusion was loved by the family for its own sake; they were twins, and born on the day sacred to Santa Magdalena. Slumbering dogs and cats were disposed about the floor, also four children. The eldest, a boy, sitting with legs outstretched before him, was cutting threads from a slip of colt's hide looped over his great toe. The two next, boy and girl, were playing a simple game called nines, once known to English children as nine men's morrice; the lines were rudely scratched on the clay floor, and the men they played with were bits of hardened clay, nine red and as many white. The youngest, a girl of five, sat on the floor nursing a kitten that purred contentedly on her lap and drowsily winked its blue eyes at the fire; and as she swayed herself from side to side she lisped out the old lullaby in her baby voice:

A-ro-ró mi niño
  A-ro-ró mi sol,
A-ro-ró pedazos
  De mi corazon.

Gregory stood on the threshold surveying this domestic scene with manifest pleasure.

"Papa mine, what have you brought me?" cried the child with the kitten.

"Brought you, interested? Stiff whiskers and cold hands to pinch your dirty little cheeks. How is your cold to-night, mother?"

"Yes, son, it is very cold to-night; we knew that before you came in," replied the old dame testily as she drew her chair a little closer to the fire.

"It is useless speaking to her," remarked Ascension. "With her to be out of temper is to be deaf."

"What has happened to put her out?" he asked.

"I can tell you, papa," cried one of the twins. "She wouldn't let me make your cigars to-day, and sat down out-of-doors to make them herself. It was after breakfast when the sun was warm."

"And of course she fell asleep," chimed in Ascension.

"Let me tell it, auntie!" exclaimed the other. "And she fell asleep, and in a moment Rosita's lamb came and ate up the whole of the tobacco-leaf in her lap."

"It didn't!" cried Rosita, looking up from her game. "I opened its mouth and looked with all my eyes, and there was no tobacco-leaf in it."

"That lamb! that lamb!" said Gregory slily. "Is it to be wondered at that we are turning grey before our time—all except Rosita! Remind me to-morrow, wife, to take it to the flock: or if it has grown fat on all the tobacco-leaf, aprons and old shoes it has eaten——"

"Oh no, no, no!" screamed Rosita, starting up and throwing the game into confusion, just when her little brother had made a row and was in the act of seizing on one of her pieces in triumph.

"Hush, silly child, he will not harm your lamb," said the mother, pausing from her task and raising eyes that were tearful with the smoke of the fire and of the cigarette she held between her good-humoured lips. "And now, if these children have finished speaking of their important affairs, tell me, Gregory, what news do you bring?"

"They say," he returned, sitting down and taking the maté-cup from his daughter's hand, "that the invading Indians bring seven hundred lances, and that those that first opposed them were all slain. Some say they are now retreating with the cattle they have taken; while others maintain that they are waiting to fight our men."

"Oh, my sons, my sons, what will happen to them!" cried Magdalen, bursting into tears.

"Why do you cry, wife, before God gives you cause?" returned her husband. "Are not all men born to fight the infidel? Our boys are not alone—all their friends and neighbours are with them."

"Say not this to me, Gregory, for I am not a fool nor blind. All their friends indeed! And this very day I have seen the Niño Diablo; he galloped past the house, whistling like a partridge that knows no care. Why must my two sons be called away, while he, a youth without occupation and with no mother to cry for him, remains behind?"

"You talk folly, Magdalen," replied her lord. "Complain that the ostrich and puma are more favoured than your sons, since no man calls on them to serve the state; but mention not the Niño, for he is freer than the wild things which Heaven has made, and fights not on this side nor on that."

"Coward! Miserable!" murmured the incensed mother.

Whereupon one of the twins flushed scarlet, and retorted, "He is not a coward, mother!"

"And if not a coward why does he sit on the hearth among women and old men in times like these? Grieved am I to hear a daughter of mine speak in defence of one who is a vagabond and a stealer of other men's horses!"

The girl's eyes flashed angrily, but she answered not a word.

"Hold your tongue, woman, and accuse no man of crimes," spoke Gregory. "Let every Christian take proper care of his animals; and as for the infidel's horses, he is a virtuous man that steals them. The girl speaks truth; the Niño is no coward, but he fights not with our weapons. The web of the spider is coarse and ill-made compared with the snare he spreads to entangle his prey." Thus fixing his eyes on the face of the girl who had spoken, he added: "therefore be warned in season, my daughter, and fall not into the snare of the Niño Diablo."

Again the girl blushed and hung her head.

At this moment a clatter of hoofs, the jangling of a bell, and shouts of a traveller to the horses driven before him, came in at the open door. The dogs roused themselves, almost overturning the children in their hurry to rush out; and up rose Gregory to find out who was approaching with so much noise.

"I know, *papita*," cried one of the children. "It is Uncle Polycarp."

"You are right, child," said her father. "Cousin Polycarp always arrives at night, shouting to his animals like a troop of Indians." And with that he went out to welcome his boisterous relative.

The traveller soon arrived, spurring his horse, scared at the light and snorting loudly, to within two yards of the door. In a few minutes the saddle was thrown off, the fore feet of the bell-mare fettered, and the horses allowed to wander away in quest of pasturage; then the two men turned into the kitchen.

A short, burly man aged about fifty, wearing a soft hat thrust far back on his head, with truculent greenish eyes beneath arched bushy eyebrows, and a thick shapeless nose surmounting a bristly moustache—such was Cousin Polycarp. From neck to feet he was covered with a blue cloth poncho, and on his heels he wore enormous silver spurs that clanked and jangled over the floor like the fetters of a convict. After greeting the women and bestowing the avuncular blessing on the children, who had clamoured for it as for some inestimable boon—he sat down, and flinging back his poncho displayed at his waist a huge silver-hilted knife and a heavy brass-barrelled horse-pistol.

"Heaven be praised for its goodness, Cousin Magdalen," he said. "What with pies and spices your kitchen is more fragrant than a garden of flowers. That's as it should be, for nothing but rum have I tasted this bleak day. And the boys are away fighting, Gregory tells me. Good! When the eaglets have found out their wings let them try their talons. What, Cousin Magdalen, crying for the boys! Would you have had them girls?"

"Yes, a thousand times," she replied, drying her wet eyes on her apron.

"Ah, Magdalen, daughters can't be always young and sweet-tempered, like your brace of pretty partridges yonder. They grow old, Cousin Magdalen—old and ugly and spiteful; and are more bitter and worthless than the wild pumpkin. But I speak not of those who are present, for I would say nothing to offend my respected Cousin Ascension, whom may God preserve, though she never married."

"Listen to me, Cousin Polycarp," returned the insulted dame so pointedly alluded to. "Say nothing to me nor of me, and I will also hold my peace concerning you; for you know very well that if I were disposed to open my lips I could say a thousand things."

"Enough, enough, you have already said them a thousand times," he interrupted. "I know all that, cousin; let us say no more."

"That is only what I ask," she retorted, "for I have never loved to bandy words with you; and you know already, therefore I need not recall it to your mind, that if I am single it is not because some men whose names I could mention if I felt disposed—and they are the names not of dead but of living men—would not have been glad to marry me, but because I preferred my liberty and the goods I inherited from my father; and I see not what advantage there is in being the wife of one who is a brawler and a drunkard and spender of other people's money, and I know not what besides."

"There it is!" said Polycarp, appealing to the fire. "I knew that I had thrust my foot into a red ant's nest—careless that I am! But in truth, Ascension, it was fortunate for you in those distant days you mention that you hardened your heart against all lovers. For wives, like cattle that must be branded with their owner's mark, are first of all taught submission to their husbands; and consider, cousin, what tears! what sufferings!" And having ended thus abruptly, he planted his elbows on his knees and busied himself with the cigarette he had been trying to roll up with his cold drunken fingers for the last five minutes.

Ascension gave a nervous twitch at the red cotton kerchief on her head, and cleared her throat with a sound "sharp and short like the shrill swallow's cry," when —

"*Madre del Cielo*, how you frightened me!" screamed one of the twins, giving a great start.

The cause of this sudden outcry was discovered in the presence of a young man quietly seated on the bench at the girl's side. He had not been there a minute before, and no person had seen him enter the room—what wonder that the girl was startled! He was slender in form and had small hands and feet, and oval olive face, smooth as a girl's except for the incipient moustache on his lip. In place of a hat he wore only a scarlet ribbon bound about his head, to keep back the glossy black hair that fell to his shoulders; and he was wrapped in a white woollen Indian poncho, while his lower limbs were cased in white coltskin coverings, shaped like stockings to his feet, with the red tassels of his embroidered garters falling to the ankles.

"The Niño Diablo!" all cried in a breath, the children manifesting the greatest joy at his appearance. But old Gregory spoke with affected anger. "Why do you always drop on us in this treacherous way, like rain through a leaky thatch?" he exclaimed. "Keep these strange arts for your visits in the infidel country; here we are all Christians, and praise God on the threshold when we visit a neighbour's house. And now, Niño Diablo, what news of the Indians?"

"Nothing do I know and little do I concern myself about specks on the horizon," returned the visitor with a light laugh. And at once all the children gathered round him, for the Niño they considered to belong to them when he came, and not to their elders with their solemn talk about Indian warfare and lost horses. And now, now he would finish that wonderful story, long in the telling, of the little girl alone and lost in the great desert, and surrounded by all the wild animals met to discuss what they should do with her. It was a grand story, even mother Magdalen listened, though she pretended all the time to be thinking only of her pies—and the teller, like the grand old historians of other days, put most eloquent speeches, all made out of his own head, into the lips (and beaks) of the various actors—puma, ostrich, deer, cavy, and the rest.

In the midst of this performance supper was announced, and all gathered willingly round a dish of Magdalen's pies, filled with minced meat, hard-boiled eggs chopped small, raisins, and plenty of spice. After the pies came roast beef; and, finally, great basins of mutton broth fragrant with herbs and cummin-seed. The rage of hunger satisfied, each one said a prayer, the elders murmuring with bowed heads, the children on their knees uplifting shrill voices. Then followed the concluding semi-religious ceremony of the day, when each child in its turn asked a blessing of father, mother, grandmother, uncle, aunt, and not omitting the stranger within the gates, even the Niño Diablo of evil-sounding name.

The men drew forth their pouches, and began making their cigarettes, when once more the children gathered round the story-teller, their faces glowing with expectation.

"No, no," cried their mother. "No more stories to-night—to bed, to bed!"

"Oh, mother, mother!" cried Rosita pleadingly, and struggling to free herself; for the good woman had dashed in among them to enforce obedience. "Oh, let me stay till the story ends! The reed-cat has said such things! Oh, what will they do with the poor little girl?"

"And oh, mother mine!" drowsily sobbed her little sister; "the armadillo that said—that said nothing because it had nothing to say, and the partridge that whistled and said,—" and here she broke into a prolonged wail. The boys also added their voices until the hubbub was no longer to be borne, and Gregory rose up in his wrath and called on someone to lend him a big whip; only then they yielded, and still sobbing and casting many a lingering look behind, were led from the kitchen.

During this scene the Niño had been carrying on a whispered conversation with the pretty Magdalen of his choice, heedless of the uproar of which he had been the indirect cause; deaf also to the bitter remarks of Ascension concerning some people who, having no homes of their own, were fond of coming uninvited into other people's houses, only to repay the hospitality extended to them by stealing their silly daughters' affections, and teaching their children to rebel against their authority.

But the noise and confusion had served to arouse Polycarp from a drowsy fit; for like a boa constrictor, he had dined largely after his long fast, and dinner had made him dull; bending toward his cousin he whispered earnestly: "Who is this young stranger, Gregory?"

"In what corner of the earth have you been hiding to ask who the Niño Diablo is?" returned the other.

"Must I know the history of every cat and dog?"

"The Niño is not cat nor dog, cousin, but a man among men, like a falcon among birds. When a child of six the Indians killed all his relations and carried him into captivity. After five years he escaped out of their hands, and, guided by sun and stars and signs on the earth, he found his way back to the Christian's country, bringing many beautiful horses stolen from his captors; also the name of Niño Diablo first given to him by the infidel. We know him by no other."

"This is a good story; in truth I like it well—it pleases me mightily," said Polycarp. "And what more, cousin Gregory?"

"More than I can tell, cousin. When he comes the dogs bark not—who knows why? his tread is softer than the cat's; the untamed horse is tame for him. Always in the midst of dangers, yet no harm, no scratch. Why? Because he stoops like the falcon, makes his stroke and is gone—Heaven knows where!"

"What strange things are you telling me? Wonderful! And what more, cousin Gregory?"

"He often goes into the Indian country, and lives freely with the infidel, disguised, for they do not know him who was once their captive. They speak of the Niño Diablo to him, saying that when they catch that thief they will flay him alive. He listens to their strange stories, then leaves them, taking their finest ponchos and silver ornaments, and the flower of their horses."

"A brave youth, one after my own heart, cousin Gregory. Heaven defend and prosper him in all his journeys into the Indian territory! Before we part I shall embrace him and offer him my friendship, which is worth something. More, tell me more, cousin Gregory?"

"These things I tell you to put you on your guard; look well to your horses, cousin."

"What!" shouted the other, lifting himself up from his stooping posture, and staring at his relation with astonishment and kindling anger in his countenance.

The conversation had been carried on in a low tone, and the sudden loud exclamation startled them all—all except the Niño, who continued smoking and chatting pleasantly to the twins.

"Lightning and pestilence, what is this you say to me, Gregory Gorostiaga!" continued Polycarp, violently slapping his thigh and thrusting his hat farther back on his head.

"Prudence!" whispered Gregory. "Say nothing to offend the Niño, he never forgives an enemy—with horses."

"Talk not to me of prudence!" bawled the other. "You hit me on the apple of the eye and counsel me not to cry out. What! have not I, whom men call Polycarp of the South, wrestled with tigers in the desert, and must I hold my peace because of a boy—even a boy devil? Talk of what you like, cousin, and I am a meek man—meek as a sucking babe; but touch not on my horses, for then I am a whirlwind, a conflagration, a river flooded in winter, and all wrath and destruction like an invasion of Indians! Who can stand before me? Ribs of steel are no protection! Look at my knife; do you ask why there are stains on the blade? Listen: because it has gone straight to the robber's heart!"

And with that he drew out his great knife and flourished it wildly, and made stabs and slashes at an imaginary foe suspended above the fire.

The pretty girls grew silent and pale and trembled like poplar leaves; the old grandmother rose up, and clutching at her shawl toddled hurriedly away, while Ascension uttered a snort of disdain. But the Niño still talked and smiled, blowing thin smoke-clouds from his lips, careless of that tempest of wrath gathering before him; till, seeing the other so calm, the man of war returned his weapon to its sheath, and glancing round and lowering his voice to a conversational tone, informed his hearers that his name was Polycarp, one known and feared by all men,—especially in the south; that he disposed to live in peace and amity with the entire human race, and he therefore considered it unreasonable of some men to follow him about the world asking him to kill them. "Perhaps," he concluded, with a touch of irony, "they think I gain something by putting them to death. A mistake, good friends; I gain nothing by it! I am not a vulture and their bodies can be of no use to me."

Just after this sanguinary protest and disclaimer the Niño all at once made a gesture as if to impose silence, and turning his face toward the door, his nostrils dilating, and his eyes appearing to grow large and luminous like those of a cat.

"What do you hear, Niño?" asked Gregory.

"I hear lapwings screaming," he replied.

"Only at a fox perhaps," said the other. "But go to the door, Niño, and listen."

"No need," he returned, dropping his hand, the light of a sudden excitement passing from his face. "'Tis only a single horseman riding this way at a fast gallop."

Polycarp got up and went to the door, saying that when a man was among robbers it behooved him to look well after his cattle. Then he came back and sat down again. "Perhaps," he remarked, with a side glance at the Niño, "a better plan would be to watch the thief. A lie, cousin Gregory; no lapwings are screaming; no single horseman approaching at a fast gallop. The night is serene, and earth as silent as the sepulchre."

"Prudence!" whispered Gregory again. "Ah, cousin, always playful like a kitten; when will you grow old and wise? Can you not see a sleeping snake without turning aside to stir it up with your naked foot?"

Strange to say, Polycarp made no reply. A long experience in getting up quarrels had taught him that these impassive men were, in truth, often enough like venomous snakes, quick and deadly when roused. He became secret and watchful in his manner.

All now were intently listening. Then said Gregory, "Tell us, Niño, what voices, fine as the trumpet of the smallest fly, do you hear coming from that great silence? Has the mother skunk put her little ones to sleep in their kennel and gone out to seek for the pipit's nest? Have fox and armadillo met to challenge each other to fresh trials of strength and cunning? What is the owl saying this moment to his mistress in praise of her big green eyes?"

The young man smiled slightly but answered not; and for full five minutes more all listened, then sounds of approaching hoofs became audible. Dogs began to bark, horses to snort in alarm, and Gregory rose and went forth to receive the late night-wanderer. Soon he appeared, beating the angry barking dogs off with his whip, a white-faced wild-haired man, furiously spurring his horse like a person demented or flying from robbers.

"Ave Maria!" he shouted aloud; and when the answer was given in suitable pious words, the scared-looking stranger drew near, and bending down said, "Tell me, good friend, is one whom men call Niño Diablo with you; for to this house I have been directed in my search for him?"

"He is within, friend," answered Gregory. "Follow me and you shall see him with your own eyes. Only first unsaddle, so that your horse may roll before the sweat dries on him."

"How many horses have I ridden their last journey on this quest!" said the stranger, hurriedly pulling off the saddle and rugs. "But tell me one thing more: is he well—no indisposition? Has he met with no accident—a broken bone, a sprained ankle?"

"Friend," said Gregory, "I have heard that once in past times the moon met with an accident, but of the Niño no such thing has been reported to me."

With this assurance the stranger followed his host into the kitchen, made his salutation, and sat down by the fire. He was about thirty years old, a good-looking man, but his face was haggard, his eyes bloodshot, his manner restless, and he appeared like one half-crazed by some great calamity. The hospitable Magdalen placed food before him and pressed him to eat. He complied, although reluctantly, despatched his supper in a few moments, and murmured a prayer; then, glancing curiously at the two men seated near him, he addressed himself to the burly, well-armed, and dangerous-looking Polycarp. "Friend," he said, his agitation increasing as he spoke, "four days have I been seeking you, taking neither food nor rest, so great was my need of your assistance. You alone, after God, can help me. Help me in this strait, and half of all I possess in land and cattle and gold shall be freely given to you, and the angels above will applaud your deed!"

"Drunk or mad?" was the only reply vouchsafed to this appeal.

"Sir," said the stranger with dignity, "I have not tasted wine these many days, nor has my great grief crazed me."

"Then what ails the man?" said Polycarp. "Fear perhaps, for he is white in the face like one who has seen the Indians."

"In truth I have seen them. I was one of those unfortunates who first opposed them, and most of the friends who were with me are now food for wild dogs. Where our houses stood there are only ashes and a stain of blood on the ground. Oh, friend, can you not guess why you alone were in my thoughts when this trouble came to me—why I have ridden day and night to find you?"

"Demons!" exclaimed Polycarp, "into what quagmires would this man lead me? Once for all I understand you not! Leave me in peace, strange man, or we shall quarrel." And here he tapped his weapon significantly.

At this juncture, Gregory, who took his time about everything, thought proper to interpose. "You are mistaken, friend," said he. "The young man sitting on your right is the Niño Diablo, for whom you inquired a little while ago."

A look of astonishment, followed by one of intense relief, came over the stranger's face. Turning to the young man he said, "My friend, forgive me this mistake. Grief has perhaps dimmed my sight; but sometimes the iron blade and the blade of finest temper are not easily distinguished by the eye. When we try them we know which is the brute metal, and cast it aside to take up the other, and trust our life to it. The words I have spoken were meant for you, and you have heard them."

"What can I do for you, friend?" said the Niño.

"Oh, sir, the greatest service! You can restore my lost wife to me. The savages have taken her away into captivity. What can I do to save her—I who cannot make myself invisible, and fly like the wind, and compass all things!" And here he bowed his head, and covering his face gave way to overmastering grief.

"Be comforted, friend," said the other, touching him lightly on the arm. "I will restore her to you."

"Oh, friend, how shall I thank you for these words!" cried the unhappy man, seizing and pressing the Niño's hand.

"Tell me her name—describe her to me."

"Torcuata is her name—Torcuata de la Rosa. She is one finger's width taller than this young woman," indicating one of the twins who was standing. "But not dark; her cheeks are rosy—no, no, I forget, they will be pale now, whiter than the grass plumes, with stains of dark colour under the eyes. Brown hair and blue eyes, but very deep blue. Look well, friend, lest you think them black and leave her to perish."

"Never!" remarked Gregory, shaking his head.

"Enough—you have told me enough, friend," said the Niño, rolling up a cigarette.

"Enough!" repeated the other, surprised. "But you do not know; she is my life; my life is in your hands. How can I persuade you to be with me? Cattle I have. I had gone to pay the herdsmen their wages when the Indians came unexpectedly; and my house at La Chilca, on the banks of the Langueyü, was burnt, and my wife taken away during my absence. Eight hundred head of cattle have escaped the savages, and half of them shall be yours; and half of all I possess in money and land."

"Cattle!" returned the Niño smiling, and holding a lighted stick to his cigarette. "I have enough to eat without molesting myself with the care of cattle."

"But I told you that I had other things," said the stranger full of distress.

The young man laughed, and rose from his seat.

"Listen to me," he said. "I go now to follow the Indians—to mix with them, perhaps. They are retreating slowly, burdened with much spoil. In fifteen days go to the little town of Tandil, and wait for me there. As for land, if God has given so much of it to the ostrich it is not a thing for a man to set a great value on." Then he bent down to whisper a few words in the ear of the girl at his side; and immediately afterward, with a simple "good-night" to the others, stepped lightly from the kitchen. By another door the girl also hurriedly left the room, to hide her tears from the watchful censuring eyes of mother and aunt.

Then the stranger, recovering from his astonishment at the abrupt ending of the conversation started up, and crying aloud, "Stay! stay one moment—one word more!" rushed out after the young man. At some distance from the house he caught sight of the Niño, sitting motionless on his horse, as if waiting to speak to him.

"This is what I have to say to you," spoke the Niño, bending down to the other. "Go back to Langueyü, and rebuild your house, and expect me there with your wife in about thirty days. When I bade you go to the Tandil in fifteen days, I spoke only to mislead that man Polycarp, who has an evil mind. Can I ride a hundred leagues and back in fifteen days? Say no word of this to any man. And fear not. If I fail to return with your wife at the appointed time take some of that money you have offered me, and bid a priest say a mass for my soul's repose; for eye of man shall never see me again, and the brown hawks will be complaining that there is no more flesh to be picked from my bones."

During this brief colloquy, and afterward, when Gregory and his women-folk went off to bed, leaving the stranger to sleep in his rugs beside the kitchen fire, Polycarp, who had sworn a mighty oath not to close his eyes that night, busied himself making his horses secure. Driving them home, he tied them to the posts of the gate within twenty-five yards of the kitchen door. Then he sat down by the fire and smoked and dozed, and cursed his dry mouth and drowsy eyes that were so hard to keep open. At intervals of about fifteen minutes he would get up and go out to satisfy himself that his precious horses were still safe. At length in rising, some time after midnight, his foot kicked against some loud-sounding metal object lying beside him on the floor, which on examination proved to be a copper bell of a peculiar shape, and curiously like the one fastened to the neck of his bell-mare. Bell in hand, he stepped to the door and put out his head, and lo! his horses were no longer at the gate! Eight horses: seven iron-grey geldings, every one of them swift and sure-footed, sound as the bell in his hand, and as like each other as seven claret-coloured eggs in the tinamou's nest; and the eighth the gentle piebald mare—the madrina his horses loved and would follow to the world's end, now, alas! with a thief on her back! Gone—gone!

He rushed out, uttering a succession of frantic howls and imprecations; and finally, to wind up the performance, dashed the now useless bell with all his energy against the gate, shattering it into a hundred pieces. Oh, that bell, how often and how often in how many a wayside public-house had he boasted, in his cups and when sober, of its mellow, far-reaching tone,—the sweet sound that assured him in the silent watches of the night that his beloved steeds were safe! Now he danced on the broken fragments, digging them into the earth with his heel; now in his frenzy, he could have dug them up again to grind them to powder with his teeth!

The children turned restlessly in bed, dreaming of the lost little girl in the desert; and the stranger half awoke, muttering, "Courage, O Torcuata—let not your heart break.... Soul of my life, he gives you back to me—on my bosom, rosa fresca, rosa fresca!" Then the hands unclenched themselves again, and the muttering died away. But Gregory woke fully, and instantly divined the cause of the clamour. "Magdalen! Wife!" he said. "Listen to Polycarp; the Niño has paid him out for his insolence! Oh, fool, I warned him, and he would not listen!" But Magdalen refused to wake; and so, hiding his head under the coverlet, he made the bed shake with suppressed laughter, so pleased was he at the clever trick played on his blustering cousin. All at once his laughter ceased, and out popped his head again, showing in the dim light a somewhat long and solemn face. For he had suddenly thought of his pretty daughter asleep in the adjoining room. Asleep! Wide awake, more likely, thinking of her sweet lover, brushing the dews from the hoary pampas grass in his southward flight, speeding away into the heart of the vast mysterious wilderness. Listening also to her uncle, the desperado, apostrophising the midnight stars; while with his knife he excavates two deep trenches, three yards long and intersecting each other at right angles—a sacred symbol on which he intends, when finished, to swear a most horrible vengeance. "Perhaps," muttered Gregory, "the Niño has still other pranks to play in this house."

When the stranger heard next morning what had happened he was better able to understand the Niño's motive in giving him that caution overnight; nor was he greatly put out, but thought it better that an evil-minded man should lose his horses than that the Niño should set out badly mounted on such an adventure.

"Let me not forget," said the robbed man, as he rode away on a horse borrowed from his cousin, "to be at the Tandil this day fortnight, with a sharp knife and a blunderbuss charged with a handful of powder and not fewer than twenty-three slugs."

Terribly in earnest was Polycarp of the South! He was there at the appointed time, slugs and all; but the smooth-cheeked, mysterious, child-devil came not; nor stranger still, did the scared-looking de la Rosa come clattering in to look for his lost Torcuata. At the end of the fifteenth day de la Rosa was at Langueyü, seventy-five miles from the Tandil, alone in his new rancho, which had just been rebuilt with the aid of a few neighbours. Through all that night he sat alone by the fire, pondering many things. If he could only recover his lost wife, then he would bid a long farewell to that wild frontier and take her across the great sea, and to that old tree-shaded stone farm-house in Andalusia, which he had left a boy, and where his aged parents still lived, thinking no more to see their wandering son. His resolution was taken; he would sell all he possessed, all except a portion of land in the Langueyü with the house he had just rebuilt; and to the Niño Diablo, the deliverer, he would say, "Friend, though you despise the things that others value, take this land and poor house for the sake of the girl Magdalen you love; for then perhaps her parents will no longer deny her to you."

He was still thinking of these things when a dozen or twenty military starlings—that cheerful scarlet-breasted songster of the lonely pampas—alighted on the thatch outside, and warbling their gay, careless winter-music told him that it was day. And all day long, on foot and on horseback, his thoughts were of his lost Torcuata; and when evening once more drew near his heart was sick with suspense and longing; and climbing the ladder placed against the gable of his rancho he stood on the roof gazing westward into the blue distance. The sun, crimson and large, sunk into the great green sea of grass, and from all the plain rose the tender fluting notes of the tinamou-partridges, bird answering bird. "Oh, that I could pierce the haze, with my vision," he murmured, "that I could see across a hundred leagues of level plain, and look this moment on your sweet face, Torcuata!"

And Torcuata was in truth a hundred leagues distant from him at that moment; and if the miraculous sight he wished for had been given, this was what he would have seen. A wide barren plain scantily clothed with yellow tufts of grass and thorny shrubs, and at its southern extremity, shutting out the view of that side, a low range of dune-like hills. Over this level ground, toward the range, moves a vast herd of cattle and horses—fifteen or twenty thousand head—followed by a scattered horde of savages armed with their long lances. In a small compact body in the centre ride the captives, women and children. Just as the red orb touches the horizon the hills are passed, and lo! a wide grassy valley beyond, with flocks and herds pasturing, and scattered trees, and the blue gleam of water from a chain of small lakes! There full in sight is the Indian settlement, the smoke rising peacefully up from the clustered huts. At the sight of home the savages burst into loud cries of joy and triumph, answered, as they drew near, with piercing screams of welcome from the village population, chiefly composed of women, children and old men.

It is past midnight; the young moon has set; the last fires are dying down; the shouts and loud noise of excited talk and laughter have ceased, and the weary warriors, after feasting on sweet mare's flesh to repletion, have fallen asleep in their huts, or lying out-of-doors on the ground. Only the dogs are excited still and keep up an incessant barking. Even the captive women, huddled together in one hut in the middle of the settlement, fatigued with their long rough journey, have cried themselves to sleep at last.

At length one of the sad sleepers wakes, or half wakes, dreaming that someone has called her name. How could such a thing be? Yet her own name still seems ringing in her brain, and at length, fully awake, she finds herself intently listening. Again it sounded—"Torcuata"—a voice fine as the pipe of a mosquito, yet so sharp and distinct that it tingled in her ear. She sat up and listened again, and once more it sounded "Torcuata!" "Who speaks?" she returned in a fearful whisper. The voice, still fine and small, replied: "Come out from among the others until you touch the wall." Trembling she obeyed, creeping out from among the sleepers until she came into contact with the side of the hut. Then the voice sounded again, "Creep round the wall until you come to a small crack of light on the other side." Again she obeyed, and when she reached the line of faint light it widened quickly to an aperture, through which a shadowy arm was passed round her waist; and in a moment she was lifted up and saw the stars above her, and at her feet dark forms of men wrapped in their ponchos lying asleep. But no one woke, no alarm was given; and in a very few minutes she was mounted, man-fashion, on a barebacked horse, speeding swiftly over the dim plains, with the shadowy form of her mysterious deliverer some yards in advance, driving before him a score or so of horses. He had only spoken half-a-dozen words to her since their escape from the hut but she knew by those words that he was taking her to Langueyü.

END

CPSIA information can be obtained
at www.ICGtesting.com
Printed in the USA
LVHW041014020323
740706LV00008B/1001

9 789356 902336